Young Learners English

Flyers

T0385792

Practice
Tests Plus Teacher's Guide

Kathryn Alevizos

Teaching not just testing

Pearson Education Limited
Edinburgh Gate
Harlow
Essex CM20 2JE
England
and Associated Companies throughout the world.

www.pearsonelt.com

First published 2012
Seventh impression 2018

ISBN: 978-1-4082-9940-1

Set in Sassoon Sans.
Printed in Great Britain by Ashford Colour Press Ltd, Gosport, Hants

Acknowledgements
The publishers and author would like to thank the following people and institutions
for their feedback and comments during the development of the material:

Drew Hyde and Semen Rostovtsev and the Frances King School of English.

Author Acknowledgements
Many thanks to Tessie and Karen for their useful advice and all their hard work. It is
much appreciated.

Illustrated by Quadrum Solutions.

Cover Image reproduced here by permission of Cambridge ESOL. This image is drawn
from the CYLE Tests Sample Papers, published by Cambridge ESOL, 2006.

Contents

The *Young Learners English Practice Tests Plus* series is aimed at students aged 7–12 years who are preparing for the Cambridge Young Learners English Tests. It consists of three levels: *Starters, Movers* and *Flyers*.

The CYLE Tests are suitable for learners of all nationalities whose first language is not English, whatever their cultural background. They cover all four language skills – reading, writing, listening and speaking and include a range of tasks which assess candidates' ability to use and communicate effectively in English. All candidates who complete their test receive an Award, which focuses not on what they *can't* do, but on what they *can* do. The award certificate has a shield score boundary which outlines individual attainment. The Cambridge Young Learners Tests are aligned with the Common European Framework of References for Language, at levels A1 and A2. They also provide an appropriate first step towards the main Cambridge ESOL exams (KET and PET).

■ Components

The components of *Young Learners English Practice Tests Plus* are:

- The **Student's Book** which contains five practice tests. Each test is divided into three sections: Listening, Reading & Writing and Speaking. Teachers may wish to use some of the tests as classroom practise activities before doing the others under exam conditions.

- The **Teacher's Book** which contains an overview and teaching tips for each part of the test; reduced pages of the Student's Book with embedded answers in place; Teaching guidelines for each test; a Speaking frame for each test giving procedures and language to use in each speaking test; 14 photocopiable worksheets with Teacher's Notes; CYLE grammar, structures and vocabulary lists. Test 1 of each level has suggested warm-up activities and worksheets. Teachers can choose when to use these: with Test 1 only or throughout all five tests.

- The **Multi-ROM** which includes the audio for the Listening tests, the audioscripts, a video of Speaking test 1 and video transcripts. The video of the Speaking test on the multi-ROM, together with the Speaking frame in the Teacher's Book, is designed to give teachers a detailed example of how to go about providing students with realistic practice for the Speaking test.

■ Flyers Listening Test

Overview

Parts (25 minutes)	What is the skills focus?	What does the child do?
1 (5 questions)	Listening for names and descriptions	Draws lines between names and people in a picture
2 (5 questions)	Listening for spellings, names and other information	Writes numbers or words in gaps
3 (5 questions)	Listening for detailed information	Matches pictures with illustrated items by writing a letter in a box
4 (5 questions)	Listening for specific information	Chooses between three options by putting a tick under the correct box
5 (5 questions)	Listening for specific information such as colours and words	Follows instructions to colour items in a picture, draw and write

Guidance

Part 1

- Students need to know the names they are likely to encounter in the test. These include the names new to Flyers (see pages 157–160) but also names from Starters and Movers.

- Encourage students to spend time looking at the picture before they listen to the dialogue. In particular, encourage them to identify differences between people who look similar or who are doing similar things.

- Make sure students have read the names around the picture before they listen to the dialogue so they know what names to expect. Remind them there is one name they do not need.

- Remind students of the importance of drawing clear lines between the names and the people in the picture.

Part 2

- Encourage students to predict what kind of information is missing before they listen to the dialogue. For example, whether it is a day of the week or a time that they need to listen out for.
- Make sure students are aware of the fact that there is likely to be a name spelt out in this part and sometimes also a telephone number. As a result, students need to be confident in recognising digits and letters of the alphabet. Some misspellings will be allowed for words that are not spelt out on the recording.

Part 3

- Remind students that there are eight pictures and so there are two that are not needed.
- Encourage students to look at the pictures before listening to the dialogue and think about how the pictures would be described in English so they can anticipate which words they are likely to hear.

Part 4

- Encourage students to spend time looking at the three pictures for each question before they listen to the dialogues. In particular, get students to think about the differences between the pictures.
- Make sure students listen to the whole of each dialogue before choosing A, B or C. The answer may come at any point in each of the dialogues and students should be reminded not to simply tick the first option they hear.
- Remind students to make their ticks very clear.
- Remind students to use the second time they hear the recording to check their answers.

Part 5

- Encourage students to spend time looking at the picture before they listen to the dialogue. In particular, encourage them to identify people or objects that are similar as these may be targeted. For example, if there are two boys in the picture, what makes them different from each other? Does one wear glasses or is one boy taller than the other? By doing this, students can predict what they may hear in the recording.
- Reassure students that they will only have to draw a very simple object and that their ability to draw well is not being tested. Quite often they will be asked to draw an object that is already in the picture and so they can copy.
- Remind students of the importance of writing clearly.

Teaching Tips

- Make sure students know what's expected of them in each part. Read the instructions and listen to the example. Pause the audio to check students understand.
- Always play the recording twice. If necessary with the first two or three tests, play the recording a third time.
- When checking answers, make use of the audioscript. Give students a copy of it and then play the recording again. Students listen and read to check their answers.

■ Flyers Reading & Writing Test

Overview

Parts (40 minutes)	What is the skills focus?	What does the child do?
1 (10 questions)	Reading and understanding definitions and copying words	Matches words to the correct definitions
2 (7 questions)	Reading and understanding sentences about a picture and writing one word answers	Writes yes / no after each sentence
3 (5 questions)	Reading and understanding a short dialogue and writing letters	Chooses the correct answer for each gap and writes the appropriate letter A-G
4 (6 questions)	Reading for detail and gist and copying words	Chooses the correct word for each gap in the text and selects the best title for the story
5 (7 questions)	Reading and understanding a story and completing sentences about it	Completes sentences about the story using 1, 2, 3 or 4 words

| 6 (10 questions) | Reading and understanding a factual text and copying words to fill the gaps | Selects the correct word for each gap in the text |
| 7 (5 questions) | Reading and understanding a short text such as a postcard or an extract from a diary | Provides an appropriate word for each gap in the text |

Guidance

Part 1

- Encourage students to read all the definitions before choosing the answers. Remind them that there are five words they won't need.
- Remind students that they will lose marks if they do not copy the words correctly. For example, if they spell the word incorrectly, leave out articles, or add unnecessary articles.

Part 2

- Encourage students to read the sentence carefully before answering the question. The whole sentence needs to be a correct description of the picture for the answer to be 'yes'.

Part 3

- Encourage students to read all the possible responses before making their choice. At first it may appear that more than one response fits a gap in the dialogue and so students need to read the different options carefully.
- Remind students that there is one response they do not need.
- Encourage students to check their answers by reading the whole dialogue to see if it makes sense.

Part 4

- Encourage students to read the whole text before choosing the answers so that they get a general idea of what the story is about.
- Remind students to look at the words that come before **and** after the gap to help them decide which word is correct.

- Encourage students to think about what part of speech the missing word is, i.e. a noun, a verb, an adverb or an adjective.

Part 5

- Remind students to copy words from the text correctly.
- Encourage students to underline the parts of the text that relate to the sentence they need to complete.

Part 6

- Encourage students to read through the text first.
- Encourage students to think about what kind of word is missing and to look at the words before and after the gap to get clues as to which word fits. The focus of this task is grammatical.

Part 7

- Encourage students to think about what kind of word is missing and to look at the text before and after the gap. The focus of the task is lexical and grammatical.
- Remind students to also think about the tense if the missing word is a verb.

Teaching Tips

- Make sure students know what's expected of them in each part. Read the instructions and the example and check students understand.
- Marks are often lost because letters and / or words are not written clearly. Students should check that their handwriting is clear and they should be given plenty of handwriting practice.
- Tell students to write only as much as is needed in each gap. Marks can be lost when students attempt to write more than is necessary, as it often leads to more mistakes being made.
- Teach your young students to manage their time well. Set time limits in class so that they can experience the limited time of the exam. This will help students concentrate and be less distracted by other things.
- Make sure students are familiar with the structures and vocabulary in the *Starters*, *Movers* and *Flyers* syllabus (see pages 156–160).

◼ Flyers Speaking Test

Overview

Parts (7-9 minutes)	What is the skills focus?	What does the child do?
1	Understanding sentences about pictures and making statements describing the differences between pictures	Identifies the six differences between his / her picture and the examiner's picture
2	Understanding and responding to questions and asking questions to gain information	Asks and answers questions about two people, situations or objects
3	Understanding the introduction of a story and then telling the rest of the story	Describes pictures in order to tell a story
4	Understanding and answering personal questions	Answers personal questions

Guidance

Part 1

- Remind students to listen carefully to what the examiner says and to try and use the same language in giving their response. For example:

  Examiner – *In my picture, there is a red book under the table.*

  Candidate – *In my picture, there is a <u>blue</u> book under the table.*

- Encourage students to respond in complete sentences.

Part 2

- Remind students that the examiner will ask the questions first and to listen to these carefully as they will need to ask the examiner the same questions. Also give them plenty practice in forming questions from prompts.

- Students need only give short answers.

Part 3

- Remind students that the examiner will ask them to look at all five pictures before they start the task and that it's a good idea for students to try and get a general idea of the story before they start. However it is also worth reassuring students that if they cannot see how the pictures link together, they can simply describe what they can see in each picture.

- Encourage students to think about the grammar they will need to use to tell the story. For example, to use present perfect for things that have already happened in the story (*they have forgotten their camera*) or present continuous for things that are happening in the picture (*they are having a picnic*).

Part 4

- Encourage students to listen carefully to the examiner's questions, but remind them that they can ask the examiner if they don't understand.

- Give students practice answering questions about themselves, their families and friends, their homes, their school, their free-time activities and their likes and dislikes.

- Only simple answers of between one to four words are expected, though encourage them to use full sentences if they can.

- Questions will normally be in the present tense but candidate should be prepared to talk about what they did in the recent past (e.g. last weekend).

Teaching Tips

- Make sure students know what's expected of them in each part. They should know that they are required to follow instructions and to talk in a very simple way about different pictures and to answers simple questions about themselves.

- Use English in class as much as possible. Students should be familiar with everyday classroom instructions. Teach them how to say *Sorry* or *I don't understand* when appropriate.

- Get students to do each speaking task in pairs before asking them to do it in front of the class.

- Give students plenty of practice doing each type of task.

- Make sure students are familiar with the structures and vocabulary in the *Starters, Movers* and *Flyers* syllabus (see pages 156–160).

Test 1

Listening Part 1

In this part, students listen and draw lines to match names to people in a picture.

■ Warm-up

Activity 1

Aim: To practise the names that appear in the Flyers test.

Materials: Sheets of paper or notebooks

Procedure

1 Write the names that may appear in the Flyers test on the board (see vocabulary list, TB page 157–160).

2 Drill the names and ask students to repeat.

3 Read out eight of the names in a random order and ask students to write them down. Check answers by getting individual students to say a name each in order.

4 Put the students in pairs. They take turns choosing four names and spelling these to their partner.

5 Remember to also revise the names from Starters and Movers.

Activity 2

Aim: To practise vocabulary for descriptions.

Materials: TB p142 Worksheet 1

Procedure

1 Put the students into pairs.

2 Give each pair the word cards from the worksheet.

3 Write the following headings on the board: 1 clothes, 2 physical appearance, 3 actions. The students group the cards into the categories, e.g. *hat* and *glasses* will go into group one, *curly* and *short* into group two, and *smiling* and *running* into group three.

4 Check the answers.

5 Ask students to draw pictures of two different people and write sentences about them using the vocabulary from the word cards.

Answer Key

Clothes: belt, shorts, striped, pocket, scarf, sweater, coat, glasses

Physical appearance: hair, blonde, beard, curly, moustache, straight, thin, fat

Actions: sitting, lying, smiling, laughing, standing, playing, running, throwing

Part 1
– 5 questions –

Listen and draw lines. There is one example.

Richard   Helen   Harry   Sarah

Paul   Katy   Robert

4   Test 1, Listening Part 1

Extension

Get students to bring in magazine pictures of people doing different things. In a small group, you could stick the pictures up around the classroom and get students to go and stand next to the person you describe. Students could then take it in turns to describe a picture to other students. In a larger group, where this may not be practical, students could work in pairs with a selection of pictures on their desk. Each student describes a person for their partner to pick out from the selection of pictures.

■ Do the test

Materials: SB page 4, Audio T1P1

1 Ask students to turn to SB page 4. Look at the picture together and get students to read the names written at the top and bottom of the picture.

2 Play the recording and pause it after the example. Go through the example with the class, making sure they understand what they need to do.

3 Play the rest of the recording. The students draw a line from the names to the appropriate people in the picture.

4 Let the students listen to the audio again. Check answers.

Audioscript

R	= Rubric
Fch	= Female child
F	= Female adult
Mch	= Male child
M	= Male adult

R **Listen and look. There is one example.**

Fch Dad! Come and look at my photos.

M OK. Oh, is this a photo of your new Art club?

Fch Yes, look – there's Richard!

M Where?

Fch There! He's standing next to the window – he's the boy with the red t-shirt.

M Oh, yes. He's holding a bottle of blue paint.

R **Can you see the line? This is an example.**

Now you listen and draw lines.

M Who's the boy who's sitting at the table next to Richard?

Fch There are two boys who're sitting at that table. Which one do you mean?

M The one with blonde hair. He's drawing a cat, I think.

Fch Oh, that's Robert. He's very good at drawing animals.

M Look at the other table. They're painting pictures of faces.

Fch Yes, they're painting people in the class.

M Who's the girl with long dark hair? Look, she's sitting next to the bookcase.

Fch That's Katy. She won the school art competition last year – she loves art.
Can you see my friend Helen? She's talking to my teacher.

M No. Where is she?

Fch She's there, near the door.

M Oh. Is she wearing glasses?

Fch No, she's the one with curly hair.

M Where's your friend, Sarah, then?

Fch Oh, she's getting some more paper from the teacher's desk.

M Is that her with the pink skirt?

Fch No, she's standing next to that girl. She's wearing green trousers. They're going to do some drawing, I think.

M Who's the boy over there? Look, he's looking for something under the table.

Fch Oh, that's Harry.

M What's he looking for?

Fch I think he dropped his pencil.

R **Now listen to Part One again.**

Answer Key ➤ SB page 4

Test 1

Listening Part 2

In this part, students listen and write words or numbers in gaps.

■ Warm-up

Activity 1

Aim: To practise the alphabet and spelling.

Materials: TB p142 Worksheet 1

Procedure

1 For this part of the Listening Test, students need to be confident about the names of the letters of the alphabet. Choose words from one of the Flyers topic sets. Play hangman with one of the words, with different students guessing letters. Then get confident students to come to the front and choose the word.

2 Give out a copy of the worksheet to each pair of pupils.

3 The students each choose five words from the word cards and take turns spelling these to their partner. They then compare and check their spellings.

Activity 2

Aim: To practise listening for and writing information (i.e. names and numbers).

Materials: TB p143 Worksheet 2

Procedure

1 Put the students into pairs.

2 Give student A a copy of Card A from the worksheet, and student B a copy of Card B.

3 They take it in turns to ask each other questions so they can fill in their form, e.g. *What time is the tennis lesson?* Go round helping where necessary.

4 They then compare the completed information exchange forms to check their answers.

Part 2
– 5 questions –

Listen and write. There is one example.

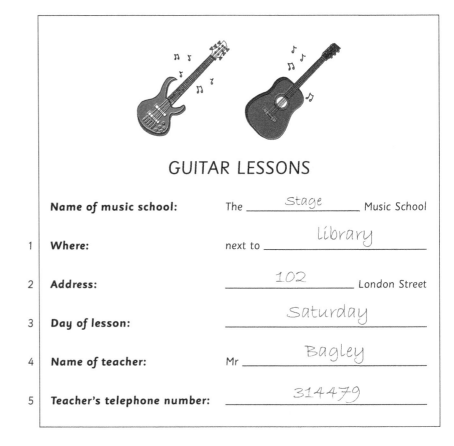

GUITAR LESSONS

Name of music school:	The ___*Stage*___ Music School	
1	Where:	next to ___*library*___
2	Address:	___*102*___ London Street
3	Day of lesson:	___*Saturday*___
4	Name of teacher:	Mr ___*Bagley*___
5	Teacher's telephone number:	___*314479*___

Test 1, Listening Part 2   5

■ Do the test

Materials: SB page 5, Audio T1P2

1 Ask students to turn to SB page 5. Look at the form together and get students to think about what kind of information is missing.

2 Play the recording and pause it after the example. Go through the example with the class, making sure they understand what they need to do.

3 Play the rest of the recording. The students listen and fill in the missing words on the form.

4 Let the students listen to the audio again. Check answers.

Audioscript

R **Listen and look. There is one example.**

F Oh hello, George. Can I ask you some questions?

M Yes, of course, Holly. What about?

F The guitar lessons which your son has. My daughter would like to learn the guitar.

M Really? Oh, my son really enjoys his guitar lessons. What do you want to know?

F Which music school does he go to?

M It's called The Stage Music School.

F Right. I think I've heard of that. Let me write it down.

M OK.

R **Can you see the answer? Now you listen and write.**

F Right. And where is it? Is it far from here?

M No, not really. It's next to the library in the town centre.

F Oh. OK.
I'm not sure where that is. What's the address again?

M It's 102 London Street.

F Right. Is that opposite the bank?

M No, that's number 101.

F What day are the guitar lessons?

M Well, the guitar teacher only works on Saturdays, but the music school is open from Tuesday to Sunday.

F Oh. That's OK. I think the weekend is better than in the week after school.

M Yes, I agree. The children aren't as tired at the weekend.

F And now what's the name of the guitar teacher?

M He's called Mr Bagley. That's spelt B-A-G-L-E-Y. He's a very nice man.

F Excellent! I'll phone the school this evening.

M Oh, you have to phone the guitar teacher, not the music school.

F Right. Do you have the teacher's phone number?

M Yes, I think so. Let me see. Oh yes. Here it is. It's three one double four seven nine.

F Thank you very much.

M That's OK. I hope your daughter enjoys her guitar lessons!

R **Now listen to Part Two again.**

Answer Key ➤ SB page 5

Listening Part 3

In this part, students listen and match pictures to words or names by writing a letter in the box.

■ Warm-up

Activity 1

Aim: To practise identifying vocabulary from pictures.

Materials: TB p144 Worksheet 3

Procedure

1 Put the students into pairs.

2 Give each pair a copy of the worksheet. Get students to take turns naming each of the items.

3 Ask them to cut out the cards. Read out a list of the items in a random order and the students put the pictures in the order they hear them. Check answers by asking students to say the words in turn.

4 With the same set of pictures, get students to turn the pictures face down on their desk. In pairs, each student picks up a picture, and without showing their partner, describes the picture for their partner to guess the word, e.g. *You can take it on holiday. It's often silver or black. (a camera)*.

Activity 2

Aim: To practise matching pictures to names.

Materials: TB p144 Worksheet 3

Procedure

1 Write the following names on the board: *Betty, David, Emma, Robert, Sarah, Michael.*

2 Place a set of the picture cards from Worksheet 3 on a table at the front of the class.

3 Say *Robert likes playing football. He practises every day. He always takes his sports bag with him when he goes.* Ask a student to come to the front and pick up the relevant picture card and place it next to the correct name, e.g. *sports bag* next to *Robert.* Ask the rest of the class if they agree.

4 Repeat with the following sentences and different students.

Sarah likes sweets but she doesn't eat them every day. Her favourite kind of sweets is chocolate.

Betty has got a new pair of socks. They are pink and blue with monkeys on them.

Michael goes to music lessons on Saturday. He's learning to play the guitar but not the piano.

It was Emma's birthday last week. I gave her a new T-shirt. It's got spots on it.

My friend David can't find his pencil case. He thinks that he lost it at school.

■ Do the test

Materials: SB pages 6 & 7, Audio T1P3

1 Ask students to turn to SB pages 6 & 7. Look at the list of words or names and the set of pictures with the class.

2 Play the recording and pause it after the example. Go through

Part 3
– 5 questions –

What birthday present did Sarah get from each person?
Listen and write a letter in each box. There is one example.

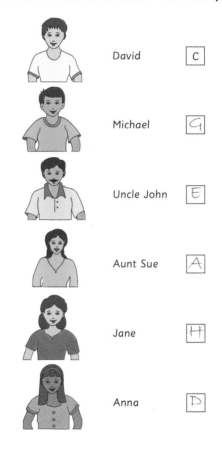

David [C]

Michael [G]

Uncle John [E]

Aunt Sue [A]

Jane [H]

Anna [D]

6   Test 1, Listening Part 3

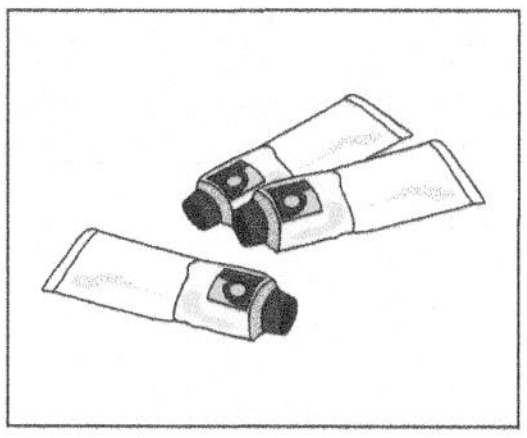

A

B

C

D

E

F

G

H

the example with the class, making sure they understand what they need to do.

3 Play the rest of the recording. The students listen and match the illustrated names with the pictures, A to H.

4 Let the students listen to the audio again. Check answers.

Audioscript

R **Listen and look. There is one example.**

What birthday present did Sarah get from each person?

F Did you enjoy your birthday, Sarah?

Fch Yes mum, it was great. I loved my party – I think everyone had a good time. I got some lovely presents this year. Look, do you like this? Cousin David bought it for me. It's a lovely t-shirt. It will look good with my white jeans. I think I'll wear it to my friend's party next week.

R **Can you see the letter 'C'? Now you listen and write a letter in each box.**

F What else did you get?

Fch Well. Aunt Sue got me some nice paints from that new supermarket in town. I could do a picture for her ... perhaps one of a rainbow. You know she loves my pictures. I'll do one tomorrow.

F Did someone give you a DVD as well?

Fch No, but I got a book from my friend Jane. It's got some great photos of elephants in it. I'm going to use it for my school project on wild animals. It'll be very useful.

F Great! ... I like this present.

Fch Yes, it was from Uncle John. They're funny socks – with monkeys on them! I don't know where he buys his presents - they're always very different! I think I'm going to wear them to school tomorrow. They will make everyone laugh!

F Yes! This present is very nice, too.

Fch Yes, I love the pencil case. Anna gave it to me. It's the same colour as my backpack. Look, I've already put all my pens and pencils in it.

F Oh, yes. And what did you get from your other cousins?

Fch Michael gave me this lovely big sports bag. It's big enough to put my basketball in. I can put my horrible old bag in the bin! I'll take it to basketball today. I love all my presents – I've had a great birthday mum!

R **Now listen to Part Three again.**

Answer Key ➤ SB page 6

Listening Part 4

In this part, students listen and tick the correct picture.

■ Warm-up

Activity 1

Aim: To raise awareness of the use of distracters (wrong answers) in listening texts.

Materials: TB p145 Worksheet 4

Procedure

1 Give out copies of the worksheet without cutting out the pictures. Ask students to look at the pictures in row 1.

2 Read out the first part of the mini-dialogue and get students to choose the correct option (*orange juice*). Elicit from students why the other two options were wrong (*Harry doesn't like milk and Mrs Brown doesn't have any lemonade*). Reread the mini-dialogue if necessary.

3 Read the other mini-dialogues. Students work together to choose the correct option and explain why the other two aren't correct. Check answers.

Mini-dialogue scripts

1 What does Harry drink?

Would you like some milk Harry?
I don't like milk Mrs Brown. Could I have some lemonade please?
I'm sorry, we haven't got any. Shall I get you some orange juice?
OK, thanks.

2 When do they need to leave?

It's 9:45 Anna, we're going to be late for your tennis lesson!
It's OK dad, it begins at quarter past ten today.
Oh, all right, but we still need to leave at ten o'clock so go and get ready.
OK, dad.

3 Where is the bag?

Did I leave my bag on the kitchen table mum?
It's not there now. Is it on the sofa?
I've looked there. Oh there it is, on the stairs. I've got it mum!
OK, Ben.

4 Who is Tom's teacher?

Is that woman with dark hair your Maths teacher, Tom?
That's my geography teacher. My maths teacher has got long blonde hair.
Oh, yes I can see her. She's wearing glasses, too.
That's right.

5 What is Jane going to wear?

Are you going to wear your red and purple dress to the party, Jane?
That's too small for me now.
Is it?
Yes, I've got a new green spotted one and mum's going to wear her new striped one.

Part 4
– 5 questions –

Listen and tick (✓) the box. There is one example.

What is William reading about?

A ☐   B ✓   C ☐

1   What will William drink with his breakfast?

 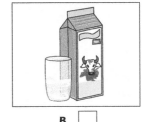 

A ✓   B ☐   C ☐

2   Where is William's History book?

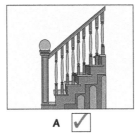 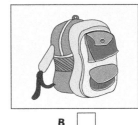 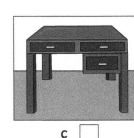

A ✓   B ☐   C ☐

Answer Key

1 orange juice   **2** 10:00
3 on the stairs   **4** long hair / glasses
5 spotted dress

Activity 2

Aim: To practise grouping sets of vocabulary.

Materials: TB p145 Worksheet 4

Procedure

1 Put the students into pairs.

2 Give each pair a set of cut-up picture cards from the worksheet.

3 The students work together to sort the picture cards into lexical sets of three. Check the answers. In their pairs they take turns naming the objects or actions depicted in each card.

3 What homework did William have?

 A ☐

 B ☐

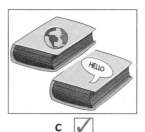 C ✓

4 Which shorts will William take to football practice?

 A ☐

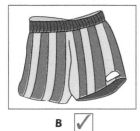 B ✓

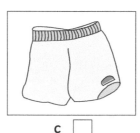 C ☐

5 What time will William see the dentist?

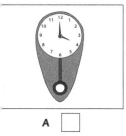 A ☐

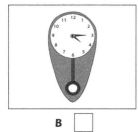 B ☐

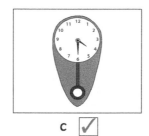 C ✓

Test 1, Listening Part 4

4 Ask them to write a description of each card to test spelling. Go round checking their answers.

■ Do the test

Materials: SB pages 8 & 9, Audio T1P4

1 Ask students to turn to SB pages 8 & 9. Look at the five questions together and get students to think about what differences they can see in each set of pictures.

2 Play the recording and pause it after the example. Go through the example with the class, making sure they understand what they need to do.

3 Play the rest of the recording. As the students listen to the questions, they look at each set of pictures and tick the correct box, A, B or C.

4 Let students listen to the audio again. Check answers.

Audioscript

R	**Listen and look. There is one example.**
	What is William reading about?
F	William, come and have some breakfast!
Mch	But I want to finish reading my magazine…
F	You're always reading about dinosaurs and monsters!
Mch	No, this is a different magazine mum, it's about big spiders! It's really interesting!
R	**Can you see the tick? Now you listen and tick the box.**

	One. What will William drink with his breakfast?
F	Well, you can finish it later. Now, do you want a glass of milk with your breakfast?
Mch	Can I have some apple juice?
F	We've only got orange juice. OK?
Mch	OK.
R	**Two. Where is William's History book?**
F	Have you put your History book in your bag?
Mch	I don't know where it is. I couldn't find it on my desk.
F	It's on the stairs. You left it there last night.
Mch	Oh, thanks.
R	**Three. What homework did William have?**
F	Did you finish your Maths and Science homework?
Mch	It was English and Geography homework mum. And yes, it's in my bag.
F	OK, good.
Mch	The homework was quite easy this week.
R	**Four. Which shorts will William take to football practice?**
F	Is that your sports bag?
Mch	Yes. I've got football practice after school today.
F	Oh, William. Why didn't you tell me? Your blue football shorts are dirty.
Mch	It's OK. I can take my green shorts.
F	They're dirty too. Here, take these striped ones.
R	**Five. What time will William see the dentist?**
F	Now remember we need to go to the dentist after school today. We need to be there at 4:30 p.m. What time does football practice finish?
Mch	At 4 o'clock.
F	OK. I'll pick you up from school at 4:15. Don't be late!
Mch	OK, mum.
R	**Now listen to Part Four again.**

Answer Key ➤ SB pages 8 & 9

Test 1, Listening Part 4   15

Listening Part 5

In this part, students listen and colour, draw and write on a picture.

■ Warm-up

Activity 1

Aim: To practise a colour dictation.

Materials: Sheets of paper or student's own notebooks, coloured pencils

Procedure

1 Revise the colours that can be used in the test using coloured pencils.

2 Draw a simple picture on the board and ask the students to copy it onto a sheet of paper or into their notebooks, e.g. a classroom with a table, a board, a map on wall, a window with a big and a small bird on the window sill, 2 desks, a girl at one with long straight hair, a girl at another with short curly hair, a bin with a pen next to it, a pen on the table.

3 Give them instructions for colouring the picture: *Colour the big bird green, Colour the map next to board blue, Colour the girl's short curly hair brown, Colour the pen next to the bin red, Colour the desk on the left orange.*

4 The students then compare drawings with a partner. Check answers by asking individual students to say an object and a colour, e.g. *a big green bird.*

Activity 2

Aim: To practise giving and following instructions for colouring, drawing and writing.

Materials: TB p146 Worksheet 5

Procedure

1 Put students into pairs.

Part 5
– 5 questions –

Listen and colour and write and draw. There is one example.

10   Test 1, Listening Part 5

2 Give each student a copy of the worksheet. Student A colours three things in picture A and then draws and writes something. Student B does the same for picture B. Give them five minutes to do this.

3 They now take turns to give their partner instructions of what to colour, draw and write. It is important that they do not show their partners their pictures so this activity is best done with students sitting back to back.

4 When they have finished, they compare their pictures to check that they look the same.

■ Do the test

Materials: SB page 10, Audio T1P5, coloured pencils

1 Ask students to turn to SB page 10. Look at the picture with the class and ask them to name items and actions in the picture. Explain that they will listen to instructions in the form of a conversation between an adult and a child.

2 Play the recording and pause it after the example. Go through the example with the class. Make sure students understand that they will need to colour three things

in the picture, write one word and draw one simple object (and also colour it).

3 Play the rest of the recording. The students listen and follow the instructions.

4 Let the students listen to the audio again. Check answers.

Audioscript

R **Listen and look at the picture.**
There is one example.

M Hello, Emma. Would you like to colour this picture?

Fch Yes please! The people are having a picnic, aren't they?

M Yes. What would you like to colour first?

Fch Umm. The woman's hair, I think.

M There are two women, but one is wearing a skirt. Colour her hair.

Fch OK. I'll colour it brown.

R **Can you see the woman's brown hair? This is an example. Now you listen and colour and write and draw.**
One

Fch What shall I colour now?

M Let's see. Can you see the girls who're sitting on the grass?

Fch Yes, I can. There are three little girls who're playing with dolls.

M Well, look at the girl on the right. She's wearing glasses.

Fch Shall I colour that girl's t-shirt green?

M OK.

R **Two**

M That's very good, but now I'd like you to write something.

Fch OK. What shall I write?

M Well, can you see the gate at the bottom of the picture?

Fch Yes, I can!

M Well, can you write the word 'ball' next to the word 'games'? Can you see the space?

Fch Yes. There! That's it.

R **Three**

M Would you like to draw something now?

Fch Yes, please. I like drawing.

M Can you see the cakes on the picnic blanket?

Fch Yes, there are three cakes on a plate.

M OK. You can draw another cake.

Fch All right. There it is.

M Now, can you colour it yellow?

Fch Fine. I'm doing that now.

R **Four**

Fch Shall I draw something else?

M No, more colouring now. There's a boy who's standing next to a tree. Can you see him?

Fch Yes.

M Well, he's flying a kite. Can you colour that?

Fch Yes. Shall I do it orange?

M No, do it red.

R **Five**

M Last thing now. There are two babies on the picnic blanket.

Fch Yes. Shall I colour the blanket?

M No, one of the babies is wearing a spotted hat. Colour it blue.

Fch OK. Is that all?

M Yes. It looks good, doesn't it?

R **Now listen to Part Five again.**

Answer Key ➤ SB page 10

Part 1
– 10 questions –

Look and read. Choose the correct words and write them on the lines.
There is one example.

a dentist   butter   a bridge   chocolate

You go to this place if you want to travel somewhere by plane.	an airport
1 This is brown and sweet. Most children like eating this.	chocolate
2 This is yellow and we put it on bread. We use it when we make cakes.	butter
3 Grown ups and children can ride this. It's got two wheels.	a bike
4 This person brings you food, usually in a restaurant or café.	a waiter
5 People go to this place if they want to catch a bus or train.	a station
6 This is white and we use it when we make cakes and sweets.	sugar
7 You should see this person if you have bad toothache.	a dentist
8 You travel in this if you need to get to hospital quickly.	an ambulance
9 This is something small we can eat if we are hungry between meals.	a snack
10 This is someone who goes into space, usually in a rocket.	an astronaut

jam   an ambulance

a waiter

a station   traffic

                                                        sugar

an astronaut   an airport   a snack

Test 1, Reading & Writing Part 1   11

Reading & Writing Part 1

In this part, students write the correct words next to the definitions.

■ Warm-up

Activity 1
Aim: To practise vocabulary.
Materials: TB p147 & 148 Worksheets 6 & 7
Procedure
1 Put the students into pairs.
2 Give each pair a copy of the worksheets and ask them to cut out the cards.

3 They work together to match the picture and word cards.
4 When they have finished, check answers.
5 They then put the word cards to one side and turn the picture cards face up on the table. Give descriptions and ask students to hold up the correct picture card, e.g. *You put a letter in this and then you put a stamp on it. (envelope).*

Activity 2
Aim: To practise matching words to definitions.
Materials: TB p148 Worksheet 7

Procedure
1 Put the students into pairs.
2 Give each pair a copy of the word cards from Worksheet 7.
3 They put these in a pile face down. Each student takes it in turn to pick up a word card and describe it for their partner to guess, e.g. *You go in this if you are ill. It takes you to hospital. (an ambulance).* If they guess correctly, they keep the card, If they are incorrect the card goes to the bottom of the pile. The winner is the student with the most cards at the end.
4 You can repeat this activity in future lessons using the picture cards from Worksheet 3.

Extension
Create a class vocabulary box: use a cardboard box and put the word cards in it. Then at the end of lessons, write any new lexis on small pieces of card and put them in the box. These words can then be used at the start or end of lessons for revision. Students can pick words from the box and either describe the word or draw the word, or even mime the word for the rest of the class to guess.

■ Do the test
Materials: SB page 11
1 Ask students to turn to SB page 11. Look at the fifteen individual words and get pupils to think about what they mean.
2 Ask students to read through the ten definitions. Look at the example together.
3 Ask the students to match the definitions with the correct words. Remind students to copy the words carefully.
4 Check the answers.

Answer Key ➤ SB page 11

Reading & Writing
Part 2

In this part, students look at a picture and then read sentences and write *yes* or *no* answers.

■ Warm-up

Activity 1

Aim: To practise listening to sentences describing a picture and deciding if they are true or false.

Materials: TB p146 Worksheet 5 (picture A)

Procedure

1 Give out copies of Picture A on the worksheet.

2 Ask simple revision questions about the picture, e.g. *What's this? What are they doing?* etc.

3 Then say statements about the picture and the students say *yes* and put their hand up if they think it is true, and say *no* if they think it is false. Count the number of hands up and check who was correct. Possible statements:

The girl wearing a dress is getting an ice cream. (yes)

The man has got a beard and a moustache. (no)

It is a cloudy day. (yes)

The girl with long hair is wearing a skirt. (no)

There are four flowers in the grass. (no)

The woman who is holding a bag is wearing a skirt. (yes)

It is a windy day and it is raining. (no)

4 You could ask confident students to come out and say statements to the class.

Activity 2

Aim: To practise writing *yes / no* answers to statements describing a picture.

Part 2
– 7 questions –

Look and read. Write yes or no.

Examples

The waiter is carrying three glasses and a bottle of water.

_____ yes _____

The woman who is talking on the telephone has got a piece of cake.

_____ no _____

Materials: TB p146 Worksheet 5 (picture B), sheets of paper or notebooks

Procedure

1 Put the students into pairs.

2 Give out copies of Picture B on Worksheet 5.

3 Each student writes five statements about the picture, some true and some false.

4 They then swap these with their partner and write *yes* or *no* about their statements.

5 Students swap statements again and correct each other's answers.

■ Do the test
Materials: SB pages 12 & 13

1 Ask students to turn to SB pages 12 & 13. Look at the picture together.

2 Ask students to look at the two examples and discuss these with the class. Ask them to correct the second example, e.g. *The woman who is talking on the telephone has got a cup / hasn't got a piece of cake.*

3 The students now decide whether the information in the other seven sentences about the picture are correct. Remind students to write

Questions

1 The man who is feeding the baby has got a beard.

_____ no _____

2 The time on the round clock is quarter to three.

_____ no _____

3 The man who is reading the newspaper is wearing glasses.

_____ yes _____

4 A boy with long blonde hair is playing with a robot.

_____ no _____

5 There is a picture of some flowers on the wall next to the clock.

_____ no _____

6 One of the men in the café is wearing a hat.

_____ no _____

7 The door which is nearer to the family is closed.

_____ yes _____

Test 1, Reading & Writing Part 2   13

either yes or no after each sentence.
Ask the students to correct the false sentences. (1 *The man who is feeding the baby hasn't got a beard. 2 The time on the clock is quarter to two. 4 A girl with long hair is playing with a doll. 5 There is a picture of some fruit on the wall next to the clock. 6 None of the men in the café is wearing a hat.*)

Answer Key ➤ SB page 13

Reading & Writing Part 3

In this part, students read a dialogue and select the correct response.

■ Warm-up

Activity 1

Aim: To practise using set formulaic expressions.

Materials: None

Procedure

1 Put the students into pairs.

2 Write the following statements/questions (1-6) on the board:

1 *Is that William's book?*

2 *What's your house like?*

3 *How long does it take to walk to school?*

4 *See you later, Vicky!*

5 *I love chocolate cake!*

6 *Have a good holiday!*

3 The students work together to predict a response for each statement or question. Do the first one as an example with the group.

4 After the pairs have made their predictions, write the following responses (A–F) on the board and ask the students to match them to 1–6 above.

5 Check their answers.

A *Me too!*

B *Thanks, you too.*

C *Yes, it is.*

D *It's big and old.*

E *See you later!*

F *About half an hour.*

Answer Key
1 C **2** D **3** F **4** E **5** A **6** B

Part 3
– 5 questions –

Ben is talking to his friend, Sam. What does Sam say?

**Read the conversation and choose the best answer.
Write a letter (A–H) for each answer.**

You do not need to use all the letters.

Example

Ben: Where are you going this weekend?

Sam: _____ E _____

Questions

1 **Ben:** Where at?

 Sam: _____ C _____

2 **Ben:** Who are you going with?

 Sam: _____ F _____

3 **Ben:** Great. Have you been camping before?

Sam: _____ A _____

4 **Ben:** I hope it doesn't rain.

Sam: _____ D _____

5 **Ben:** Have a good time.

 Sam: _____ H _____

14 Test 1, Reading & Writing Part 3

Activity 2

Aim: To practise identifying the correct sequence of a dialogue.

Materials: TB p149 Worksheet 8

Procedure

1 Cut up the three mini-dialogues on Worksheet 8.

2 Put the students into pairs and give each pair the first cut-up dialogue and keep the other dialogues on your desk.

3 Each pair must order the dialogue. When they think they have put it in the correct order, one student from the pair goes to the teacher to collect the second dialogue. This will avoid students mixing up the different dialogues.

4 At the end of the activity, each pair should have the three dialogues laid out in front of them on their table. This activity works well as a race, with the winning students being the pair who completes all three dialogues correctly first. Check answers by asking different pairs to read out their dialogues.

A   No never. I'm really excited.

B   No. I'm not happy.

C   In the forest near here.

D   Me too! My dad says it will be sunny this weekend.

E   We're going camping.   **(Example)**

F   With my dad and my brother.

G   Will you go in the sea?

H   Thanks a lot.

■ Do the test

Materials: SB pages 14 & 15

1 Ask students to turn to SB pages 14 & 15. Look at the gapped dialogue together and get students to think about what could go in the gaps.

2 Ask students to read the missing lines of the dialogue, options A–H.

3 Ask students to choose the appropriate line of dialogue from the options given and to write the correct letter in the space provided. Remind students that there is one extra line of dialogue that is not needed. Encourage them to read through the dialogue, quietly to themselves, to check that it makes sense.

4 Check answers.

Answer Key ➤ SB page 14

Reading & Writing Part 4

In this part, students choose and copy missing words from a story and then choose the best title.

■ Warm-up

Activity 1

Aim: To practise identifying different types of words.

Materials: TB p150 Worksheet 9 (top part)

Procedure

1 Write these three headings on the word: *verbs, nouns, adjectives*. Get students to suggest words to write under each heading and then write them on the board in the correct category.

2 Put the students into pairs and give out the word cards from the top part of Worksheet 9.

3 Ask students to sort the words into the three categories. Check the answers.

Extension

Store the word cards in your vocabulary box.

Activity 2

Aim: To practise filling in gaps in a text.

Materials: TB p150 Worksheet 9 (bottom part)

Procedure

1 Give out the worksheets. Ask students to read the text (bottom part of worksheet) and decide which part of speech is needed in each gap and elicit the reasons for this. For example, a verb is needed in the sentence, '*I _____ a scarf out of my rucksack*'. We know this because of the pronoun before the gap and the noun after the gap. This should help students

develop better techniques for completing this kind of task.

2 Ask them to predict words that could go in the gaps. Write their suggestions on the board.

3 They now work in pairs, look at the word cards from the worksheet and decide which one should go in which gap.

4 Check answers.

Answer Key

1 pulled 2 chopsticks
3 excellent 4 tights 5 brushing
6 broke 7 friendly 8 insects

Part 4
– 6 questions –

Read the story. Choose a word from the box. Write the correct word next to numbers 1–5. There is one example.

Last Saturday I went shopping with my mum and my sister. We were very tired after the

shopping, so mum took us to a café for a drink and a piece of _____ *cake*

Just before we left the café, I **(1)** _____ *saw* a handbag on the floor

under my chair. I showed it to my mum. She said, "You should give it to the man

who works in the café". So, I went to the waiter and gave him the handbag.

He took it and asked for my **(2)** _____ *name* and telephone number.

A **(3)** _____ *week* later the telephone rang. My mum called to me,

"Daisy, there's a woman on the phone for you. Her name's Mrs White." I was

(4) _____ *surprised* because I didn't know anyone called Mrs White.

I took the phone and spoke to the woman. The handbag I found in the café was

Mrs White's! She was very happy to have her handbag back and asked for my

(5) _____ *address* . Two days later I got a thank you letter from

Mrs White with some money!

16 Test 1, Reading & Writing Part 4

Extension

Give students more practice in this kind of task by photocopying short stories or articles from course books, graded readers and ELT newspapers and blanking out words.

■ Do the test

Materials: SB pages 16 & 17

1 Ask students to turn to SB pages 16 & 17. Look at the picture together and get students to think about the topic of the story.

Example				
cake	early	caught	saw	name
called	surprised	address	week	interesting

(6) **Now choose the best name for the story.**

Tick one box

Mrs White's handbag   ✓

The best café   ☐

My terrible day   ☐

2 Look at the example with the class and make sure they understand that they need to fill the gaps in the text from the words in the box. Remind pupils that there are more words than they need.

3 Ask students to fill in the five gaps in the story and to choose the best title for the story from the three options.

4 Check answers.

Answer Key ➤ SB pages 16 & 17

Reading & Writing Part 5

In this part, students complete sentences about a story using one, two or three words.

◼ Warm-up

Activity 1

Aim: To practise completing sentences.

Materials: None

Procedure

1 Write sentences on the board with gaps in them, e.g.

John has _____
called Mary.

Emma got the doll when she
_____ .

The park was full of people because _____ .

Harry and Robert
_____ *after lunch.*

When they were at the zoo, they
_____ .

I went _____ *last year.*

2 Ask students to work in pairs to suggest how to complete the gaps. Remind them they can use between 1 and 4 words for each, e.g. the first sentence could have *a sister, a cousin, a little sister,* etc.

3 Ask students to compare their answers by reading out a few of their sentences.

Activity 2

Aim: To practise rewording sentences.

Materials: TB p151 Worksheet 10

Procedure

1 To help students with this part of the test, it's a good idea to give them practice in recognising how sentences can be changed whilst still retaining the same meaning.

2 Put the students into pairs and give them the worksheets. Ask students to work together to fill in the gaps so that each pair of sentences has the same meaning.

3 Check answers by asking students to read out the sentences.

Answer Key

1 a brother **2** chocolate ice cream **3** their kite **4** angry **5** late **6** said sorry

◼ Do the test

Materials: SB pages 18 & 19

1 Ask students to turn to SB pages 18 & 19. Look at the picture and get students to think about the topic of the story.

2 Ask students to read the story and then read the sentences. Then ask the students to underline the parts of the story that give them the information they need to complete the sentences.

3 Look at the example with the class and make sure they understand that they need to

---

Part 5
– 7 questions –

Look at the picture and read the story. Write some words to complete the sentences about the story. You can use 1, 2, 3 or 4 words.

My first day at school

My name's Betty Stewart and I'm an English teacher. I was twenty two years old when I got my first teaching job. I remember my first day very well!

The day didn't start well. I got up early and got dressed. Then I dropped my cup of tea all over my new skirt. I quickly put on clean clothes. I picked up my bag and went to the bus stop. I saw a lot of people waiting for the bus. I asked a woman, "Why are there so many people?" She said "There's a lot of traffic in the city centre and all the buses are late." So, I decided to walk to school.

I only had half an hour before my first lesson. I walked very quickly. After some time I could see the school at the end of the road. I felt very happy. Suddenly it started to rain. I ran fast, but I was very wet when I arrived at school. When I got to my classroom I was five minutes late and I looked wet and horrible. At first, my new students looked surprised when they saw me. Then they all smiled and said, "Good morning Miss Stewart!" I smiled back and said "Good morning class!" After that, the day got much better.

18   Test 1, Reading & Writing Part 5

Examples

Betty's job is a _____teacher_____ .

She started teaching ___twenty two years___ ago.

Questions

Betty couldn't wear her new skirt to school because it had
_____tea_____ on it.

There were so _____many_____ people waiting for the bus.

There was a lot of traffic in the city centre so all the
buses ___were late___ .

Betty was _____happy_____ when she could see the school.

Before Betty arrived at school it ___started to___ rain.

When the students first saw their new teacher they
looked ___surprised___ .

Everyone in the class _____smiled_____ at Mrs Stewart and
said "Good morning".

fill the gapped sentences using
between one and four words.
Remind the students that the
words they will need to use
will be in the story but may
not be in the same order as
the sentence.

4 Ask students to complete the
gapped sentences.

5 Check the answers.

Answer Key ➤ SB page 19

Reading & Writing
Part 6

In this part, students complete a text by selecting and copying the correct words.

■ Warm-up

Activity 1

Aim: To practise predicting missing words.

Materials: TB p152 Worksheet 11

Procedure

1 Put the students into pairs.

2 Give each pair a copy of the top part of the worksheet.

3 The students work together to predict which type of word is missing in each gap, i.e. verbs, conjunctions, adverbs, etc. Encourage students to also guess the missing word if they can.

4 Write their suggestions on the board.

5 Now give each pair a copy of the bottom part of the worksheet. Ask students to select the correct word for each gap in the text.

Answer Key
1 much **2** eat **3** need **4** is
5 the **6** your **7** every **8** to
9 When **10** look

Activity 2

Aim: To raise awareness of different word groups.

Materials: None

Procedure

1 Write the following headings on the board: Verbs, Adverbs, Adjectives, Articles, Pronouns, Conjunctions.

2 Write the following words on the board: *have, never, smallest, bought, quickly, easier, are, she, then, the, opposite, best, can,*

since, dark, a, him, because, an, everyone, if, their, so.

3 Ask groups to sort the words according to what part of speech they are.

4 Check answers together, by getting members of different groups to come out and write a word each under the correct heading.

Part 6
– 10 questions –

Read the text. Choose the right words and write them on the lines.

Firemen

Example	A fireman's job is very important and _____ *each* _____ day is
1	always different. Often firemen _____ *help* _____ people who
	have a fire in their house. Other times, the fire is in a factory or
2	an office. A fire _____ *can* _____ grow very fast and so it is
3	important that the team of firemen work very _____ *quickly* _____ .
4	In the past _____ *this* _____ job was only for men, but of
5	course now there are women _____ *who* _____ work at fire
6	stations. When _____ *someone* _____ calls a fire station, a team
7	of about five firemen and women get _____ *into* _____ a
8	fire engine and drive to where the fire _____ *is* _____ .
	The driver of the fire engine must drive very fast, but carefully.
	To be a fireman or firewoman you need to be brave because it can
9	be _____ *a* _____ very dangerous job. You can't be afraid
10	of climbing and you need to be strong _____ *because* _____ you
	will sometimes carry heavy things.

20   Test 1, Reading & Writing Part 6

Answer Key

Verbs	**Adverbs**
have	never
are	opposite
bought	quickly
can	since
Adjectives	**Articles**
smallest	a
best	an
easier	the
dark	
Pronouns	**Conjunctions**
him	because
she	then
everyone	if
their	so

Example	all	each	any
1	help	helps	helping
2	need	can	should
3	quick	quicker	quickly
4	these	this	those
5	who	how	what
6	no-one	someone	everyone
7	into	onto	over
8	is	are	be
9	a	an	the
10	so	because	but

Extension

For more practice at completing gapped texts, look for short texts, or write your own short texts and blank out words for students to fill in. Give them a choice of three words for each gap.

■ Do the test

Materials: SB pages 20 & 21

1 Ask students to turn to SB pages 20 & 21. Look at the picture and get students to think about the topic of the text.

2 Go through the example.

3 Ask students to read the text and then read the word options.

4 Ask students to complete the gaps with a word.

5 Check the answers.

Answer Key ➤ SB page 20

Reading & Writing
Part 7

In this part, students complete a text with words of their own choice.

■ Warm-up

Activity 1

Aim: To practise common collocations.

Materials: TB p153 Worksheet 12

Procedure

1 As common collocations are often targeted in this part of the test, it is a good idea to give students practice in this area. Put the students into pairs.

2 Give out the worksheet and ask them to match the two halves of the phrases. They then match the phrase to a picture. Check answers.

3 After they have done this, ask students to write sentences that contain each of the collocations. Encourage them to write sentences in both the past and the present. Get individual students to read out a sentence each.

Answer Key

1 take a photo *d*
2 get on a bus *a*
3 meet a friend *f*
4 send a letter *i*
5 do homework *h*
6 make a mistake *c*
7 ride a bike *e*
8 win a race *g*
9 guess the answer *j*
10 watch TV *b*

Activity 2

Aim: To practise predicting missing words.

Materials: TB p154 Worksheet 13 (top part)

Procedure

1 Put the students into pairs.

2 Give each pair a copy of the top part of the worksheet.

3 The students work together to fill in the gaps in the text.

4 Check answers together.

Answer Key

1 having
2 you
3 at
4 can
5 of

■ Do the test

Materials: SB page 22

1 Ask students to turn to SB page 22. Look at the gapped text together and get students to think about what sort of words are missing.

2 Look at the example together and ask students to identify whether it is a noun, verb, adjective, etc.

3 Ask students to complete each gap in the text with the missing word.

4 Check answers.

Answer Key ➤ SB page 22

Part 7
– 5 questions –

Read the letter and write the missing words. Write one word on each line.

Tuesday 23ʳᵈ July

Dear Grandma,

Example We're _____ *having* _____ a good time on holiday.

Our hotel is great. I've got a big room and I can see the

1 sea _____ *from* _____ my window! Yesterday we visited

2 a castle. I _____ *took* _____ lots of photos with my

3 camera. The castle was very _____ *old* _____ and we

4 heard lots of interesting stories _____ *about* _____ the

kings and queens who lived there. It's hot and sunny today so

5 we're _____ *going* _____ to go to the beach this afternoon.

See you soon.

Lots of love,

Sarah

22 Test 1, Reading & Writing Part 7

Candidate's copy

Part 1

Find the differences

DUSTBIN

Speaking Part 1

In this part, students identify and describe differences between two pictures.

■ Warm-up

Activity 1

Aim: To practise describing pictures.

Materials: TB p155 Worksheet 14

Procedure

1　Put the students into pairs.
2　Give each pair a copy of the <u>same</u> picture from the worksheet.
3　The students each write five true or false statements about their picture. These statements should relate to things like number, colour, position, appearance, activity.
4　They then take turns to read their statements to each other. Their partner responds by saying *true* or *false*. If it is 'false', they must tell their partner how the picture is different.

Activity 2

Aim: To describe differences between two pictures.

Materials: TB p155 Worksheet 14

Procedure

1　The best preparation for this part of the test is to give students lots of practice in doing 'spot the difference' tasks.
2　Put the students into pairs.
3　Give out the worksheets: Picture A to student A and Picture B to student B. Get them to take it in turns to make statements about their picture, e.g. *In my picture there's a girl wearing a T-shirt sitting in a tree.* Their partner responds by saying how their picture is different, *In my picture the girl is wearing a jacket.* It is important that students can't see each other's pictures and so it is best if they sit back to back.

■ Do the test

Materials: SB page 24, TB page 132

1　Ask the students some general introductory questions, e.g. *What's your surname? How old are you?*
2　Ask the students to turn to SB page 24. Give them time to look at the picture.
3　Turn to the Examiner's copy (TB page 132). Allow students to look at it briefly.
4　Make statements about your copy of the picture. Encourage the student to say how their picture is different. For example, *In my picture, there is a red rucksack. (In my picture, there is a blue rucksack.)*

Answer Key

1　two elephants / one elephant
2　woman taking photo / man taking photo
3　girls eating ice cream / girls eating sandwiches
4　red rucksack / blue rucksack
5　baby is crying / baby is sleeping
6　dog is behind the bin / dog is in front of the bin
7　old woman reading a book / looking in a bag

Test 1

Speaking Part 2

In this part, students ask and answer questions using cues.

■ Warm-up

Activity 1

Aim: To practise making up questions from prompts.

Materials: None

Procedure

1 Write the following prompts on the boards: *teacher / age, How many / animals.* Encourage the students to suggest what the questions could be (they should use the present tense): *How old is the teacher? / What's the teacher's age? How many animals are there in the picture?*

2 Continue by writing these prompts and the students write the questions.

What time / football match / finish

What / boy / studying

How many / children / park

Film / interesting / boring

How long / lesson

Dog / running / jumping

3 Check the answers.

> **Answer Key**
>
> What time does the football match finish?
>
> What is the boy studying?
>
> How many children are there in the park?
>
> Is the film interesting or boring?
>
> How long is the lesson / does the lesson last?
>
> Is the dog running or jumping?

4 Ask confident students to come up and write question prompts on the board for the others to complete.

Activity 2

Aim: To practise making up and answering questions.

Materials: Paper or notebooks

Procedure

1 Write the following jumbled questions on the board:

Robert / to the party / did / with / Who / go

the / was / Where / party

go / to / party / How / Robert / did / the

dance / the / Did / party / at / Robert

the / boring / party / Was / fun / or

2 Give students a limited time to write the questions in their notebooks. Check the answers.

> **Answer Key**
>
> Who did Robert go to the party with?
>
> Where was the party?
>
> How did Robert go to the party?
>
> Did Robert dance at the party?
>
> Was the party fun or boring?

3 Put the students into pairs. Tell students that student A will make up answers for a girl called Vicky and student B will make up answers for a

Part 2

Candidate's copy

Information exchange

Harry's book

Who / gave	friend
Name / book	
What / about	Silver boots
When / finish	A footballer
Interesting / boring	yesterday
	boring

Sarah's book

Who / gave	
Name / book	
What / about	
When / finish	
Interesting / boring	

Part 3

Examiner's and Candidate's copy

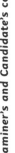

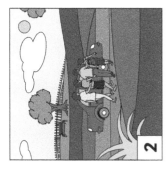
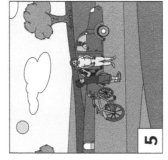

Tell the story

26 Test 1, Speaking Part 3

Speaking Part 3

In this part, students continue a story by describing the pictures in sequence.

■ Warm-up

Activity 1

Aim: To practise describing pictures.

Materials: TB p 146 Worksheet 5

Procedure

1 Put the students into pairs and give each pair one of the pictures from Worksheet 5.

2 They take it in turn to describe what is happening in the picture using the present tense, *There is / are, have got / be, can / can't, must / mustn't,* etc.

3 You could repeat this activity in another lesson using Worksheet 14.

Activity 2

Aim: To practise making up stories.

Materials: TB p154 Worksheet 13 (bottom part)

Procedure

1 Put students into groups of three and give each group one of the pictures and a story title from the worksheet.

2 Each group must decide and write down how the story continues. They then draw four more pictures to complete their story.

3 After they have done this, they come to the front, hold up their pictures and tell the rest of the class their story.

Extension

Students could draw a simple set of five pictures for homework. In the next lesson, put the students into pairs so they can tell each other their story. After they have

---

boy called William. Students write their answers to the five questions in their notebook and then take it in turns to ask each other the questions. Remind students that they will have to change the name 'Robert' in questions 1, 3 and 4 to either Vicky or William.

■ Do the test

Materials: SB page 25, TB page 133

1 Ask students to turn to SB page 25. Give them time to look at the pictures and the tables.

2 Look at the Examiner's copy (TB page 133). Ask the student questions about the information they have, e.g. *I don't know anything about Harry's book. What's the book called? (Silver Boots).*

3 Now encourage the student to ask you similar questions: *Who gave Sarah the book? What's it called?*

Answer Key ➤ Speaking frame page 35

done this, they swap pictures so that they tell their partner's story to another student in the class. This can be repeated a few times to create lots of speaking practice.

■ Do the test
Materials: SB page 26

1 Ask students to turn to SB page 26. Give them time to look at the pictures first.
2 Tell them the title and then describe the first picture, e.g. *These pictures tell a story.*
   It's called 'The camera'. There is a family having who are having a picnic. etc.
3 Encourage the students to continue the story by describing the other pictures in turn. If necessary prompt them with a question.

Answer Key ➤ Speaking frame page 35

Speaking Part 4

In this part, students answer questions about themselves, their hobbies and their family or friends.

■ Warm-up
Activity 1
Aim: To practise personal vocabulary.
Materials: Sheets of paper
Procedure
1 Put students into groups of four and give each group a large sheet of paper.

2 Then give each group a topic, e.g. *my home, hobbies, shopping, my best friend, my school,* etc. Each group draws a circle in the middle of their paper with the topic word inside it. They then create a spidergram by drawing lines from the circle and writing questions relating to the topic.
3 Students leave their sheets on their tables and get into pairs. The pairs move around the room asking each other questions from the spidergrams on each table. These spidergrams can then be saved and brought out again at the start of lessons to be used as warm-up activities.

Activity 2
Aim: To practise a role play with personal questions.
Materials: None
Procedure
1 Ask a confident student to come up to the front and demonstrate the following simple role play:
   T: *Hello, (name).*
   S: *Hello, (name).*
   T: *What time do you get up on Sunday?*
   S: *9.30.*
   T: *What do you do on Sunday afternoon?*
   S: *I go to the park.*
   T: *What are you going to do this Sunday?*
   S: *(I'm going to) visit my grandparents.*
   T: *Do you like music?*
   S: *Yes.*

   T: *Can you play an instrument?*
   S: *Yes, I can play the piano.*
   T: *Great. Thank you.*
   S: *Thanks.*

2 Put the students in pairs and ask them to do a similar role play, taking it in turns to be the teacher and the student. Encourage them to ask different questions and to add extra questions if they can. If necessary, write example questions on the board or tell them to refer to the questions from Warm-up Activity 1.
3 Go round monitoring and helping where necessary.
4 Ask a few pairs to come to the front and demonstrate their role play.

■ Do the test
Materials: None

1 Ask the students several questions about themselves, their family or friends. They need only give simple answers, i.e. a phrase or a short sentence.
   Now let's talk about your weekend
   What time do you wake up on Saturdays?
   Who makes breakfast on Saturdays?
   etc.

Speaking frame   (Timing = 7–9 minutes)

What to do	What to say	Answer from candidate	Back up question if necessary
	Hello... my name's ... *What's your surname?* *How old are you?*	Hello (Fischer) (11)	*What's your family name?* *Are you (11)?*
1 Show candidate both Find the Differences pictures. Point to the elephants in each picture.	*Here are two pictures. My picture is nearly the same as yours, but some things are different.* *For example, in my picture there are two elephants, but in your picture there's one.* *I'm going to say something about my picture. You tell me how your picture is different.* *In my picture, the girls are eating ice creams.* *In my picture, a woman's taking a photo.* *In my picture, the baby is crying.* *In my picture, there is a red rucksack.* *In my picture, there is a dog sitting behind the bin.* *In my picture, the old woman is reading a book.*	In my picture, the girls are eating sandwiches. In my picture, a man's taking a photo. In my picture, the baby is sleeping. In my picture, there is a blue rucksack. In my picture, there is a dog sitting in front of the bin. In my picture, the old woman is looking in her bag.	Point to the other differences which the student does not mention. *What are the girls eating?* *Is it a man taking a photo?* *Is the baby crying?* *Is the rucksack red?* *Where is the dog sitting?* *Is the old woman reading a book?*
2 Point to both candidate's and examiner's copies. Point to the picture of the boy before asking the questions. Point to the picture of the girl.	*Sarah and Harry have both got new books. I don't know anything about Harry's book, but you do. So I'm going to ask you some questions.* *What's the book called?* *Who gave it him?* *What's it about?* *Was it interesting or boring?* *When did he finish it?* *Now you don't know anything about Sarah's book, so you ask me some questions.* (Her cousin) (The Star) (a singer) (Last week) (interesting)	Silver Boots A friend A footballer Boring Yesterday Who gave her the book? What's it called? What's it about? When did he finish it? Was it interesting or boring?	Point to the information if necessary. Point to the information if necessary.
3 Point to the picture story. Allow time to look at the pictures.	*These pictures tell a story.* *It's called 'The camera'. Just look at the pictures first.* *There is a family who are having a picnic. The father is taking a photo of the mother and the two children. They all look very happy.* *Now you tell the story.*	2 – The family is going back to their car. They have forgotten the camera / They have left the camera on the grass. 3 – A boy on a bicycle has found the camera. He can see the family and is trying to call them / and is waving at them. The family hasn't seen him. 4 – The boy is following the car on his bicycle. The car isn't stopping. The boy is hot and tired because he going very fast on his bicycle. 5 – The car has stopped and the boy is giving the woman the camera. The woman and boy are smiling. The woman looks very happy.	*What is the family doing?* *Have they got their camera?* *Who has found the camera?* *What is the boy doing?* *Has the family seen him?* *What is the boy doing?* *Has the car stopped?* *How does the boy feel?* *Has the car stopped?* *What is the boy doing now?* *How does the woman feel?*
4 Put away all pictures. Ask a few personal questions.	*Now let's talk about your weekend.* *What time do you wake up on Saturdays?* *Who makes breakfast on Saturdays?* *What do you do with your family on Saturdays?* *Where do you go on Sundays?* *Tell me about what you like to do on Saturday evenings.* *OK, thank you (name).* *Goodbye.*	Nine My dad We go swimming We visit my grandparents. I like to watch TV. I like to eat pizza. I like to go to bed late. Goodbye.	*Do you wake up early?* *Do you make breakfast on Saturdays?* *Do you go shopping with your family?* *Do you visit family?* *Do you like to watch TV?* *What do you like to eat?* *Do you go to bed early?*

Listening Part 1

In this part, students listen and draw lines to match names to people in a picture.

■ Warm-up

For suggested warm-up activities, see Test 1 page 8.

■ Do the test

Materials: SB page 28, Audio T2P1

1 Ask students to turn to SB page 28. Look at the picture together and get students to read the names.

2 Play the recording and pause it after the example. Go through the example with the class.

3 Play the rest of the recording. The students draw a line from the names to the appropriate people in the picture.

4 Let the students listen to the audio again. Check answers.

Audioscript

R **Listen and look. There is one example.**

Fch I took this photo on my skiing holiday. Do you want to have a look?

M Yes, please. Did you have a good time?

Fch Yes, it was great. Can you see that boy who's wearing the orange jacket?

M The one who's skiing really fast down the hill?

Fch Yes. He's my brother. He's called George.

R **Can you see the line? This is an example. Now you listen and draw lines.**

M Who's that girl skiing behind him?

Fch There are two girls. Which one do you mean?

M The one with the pink hat. She looks very happy.

Fch Oh, that's our cousin, Katy. She's always smiling!

M Look at that man at the bottom of the hill, sitting in

Part 1
– 5 questions –

Listen and draw lines. There is one example.

Ben   Holly   George   Katy

Fred   Betty   Alex

28   Test 2, Listening Part 1

the snow. I think he's just fallen over.

Fch That's Fred!

M Was he skiing?

Fch No, it was his first time snowboarding.
Can you see my friend Betty? She's talking to her mum.

M No. Where is she?

Fch She's there, near the snowman.

M Oh, is she the short girl?

Fch No, she's the tall one with short hair.

M And the shorter one?

Fch Oh that's her sister. I don't know her very well.

M What about the boys throwing snowballs?

Fch The one with glasses is called Ben.

M He's a bit naughty!

Fch Yes, he threw a snowball at the ski teacher!

M Really?
Who's the other boy with blonde hair on the sledge?

Fch Oh, that's his younger brother Alex.

M It looks like a fun holiday!

Fch It was!

R **Now listen to Part One again.**

Answer Key ➤ SB page 28

Part 2
– 5 questions –

Listen and write. There is one example.

SCHOOL VISIT TO THEATRE

Day:		Thursday
1	**Time leave school:**	2.15 / two fifteen p.m.
2	**Name:**	'Guess the song'
3	**Write name on list in:**	the (school) library
4	**Give money to:**	Mr Neale
5	**Remember to take:**	some money

Listening Part 2

In this part, students listen and write words or numbers in gaps.

■ Warm-up

For suggested warm-up activities see Test 1 page 10.

■ Do the test

Materials: SB page 29, Audio T2P2

1 Ask students to turn to SB page 29. Look at the form together and get students to think about what kind of information is missing.

2 Play the recording and pause it after the example. Go through the example with the class.

3 Play the rest of the recording. The students listen and fill in the missing words on the form.

4 Let the students listen to the audio again. Check answers.

Audioscript

R **Listen and look. There is one example.**

Fch Oh hello, Miss Gray. Can I ask you some questions?

F Yes, of course, Daisy. What do you want to know?

Fch What time are we going to the theatre on Wednesday?

F Oh, didn't you know? It's on Thursday now.

Fch Oh, right.

F The football team need the school bus that day.

Fch Oh, OK

R **Can you see the answer? Now you listen and write.**

Fch What time are we going to go to the theatre?

F Well, we need to be at the theatre for 2:45 and so we're going to leave school at 2:15. The theatre isn't far from the school.

Fch OK. What are we going to see?

F It's a concert.

Fch Oh, is it called 'Guess the song'?

F Yes, that's right.

Fch I'd like to go. What do I need to do?

F You need to write your name on a list today. It's in the school library. Just write your name and your class.

Fch OK. And who do I get the ticket from?

F Mr Neale. You can give him the money on the day.

Fch Sorry, who?

F Mr Neale. That's N-E-A-L-E. He's the new music teacher.

Fch Oh, yes I've met him. Is he taking us to the theatre?

F Yes, he is.

Fch Do I need to take anything to the theatre?

F Just some money to buy a drink. Remember you cannot take your camera or your mobile phone with you.

Fch Right, OK. Are you going to come with us Miss Gray?

F Yes, I am.

Fch Great!

R **Now listen to Part Two again.**

Answer Key ➤ SB page 29

Listening Part 3

In this part, students listen and match pictures to words or names by writing a letter in the box.

■ Warm-up

For suggested warm-up activities, see Test 1 page 12.

■ Do the test

Materials: SB pages 30 & 31, Audio T2P3

1 Ask students to turn to SB pages 30 & 31. Look at the list of illustrated words and the set of pictures with the class.

2 Play the recording and pause it after the example. Go through the example with the class, making sure they understand what they need to do.

3 Play the rest of the recording. The students listen and match the illustrated words with the pictures, A to H.

4 Let the students listen to the audio again. Check answers.

Audioscript

R	**Listen and look. There is one example.** **Where did Harry get these things?**
F	Did you have a nice holiday Harry?
Mch	Yes, grandma, it was great. Look, I got some things from the different places we visited. We went to a castle one day, and dad bought me and Ben a kite each from the shop there. It was a very windy day, so we had a lot of fun flying them in the park next to it.
R	**Can you see the letter 'B'? Now you listen and write a letter in each box.**
Mch	Do you like this hat grandma?

Part 3
– 5 questions –

Where did Harry get these things?

Listen and write a letter in each box. There is one example.

kite	B
postcard	D
hat	G
T-shirt	H
chocolates	F
pen	E

30   Test 2, Listening Part 3

F	Oh yes, that's lovely. What does it say on the front of it?
Mch	Blue Dolphin. It's the name of the boat we went on when we visited Parrot Island. But there weren't any shops on the Island, so I got it on the boat. It was a great day!
F	And did you visit the zoo?
Mch	We wanted to but it was closed so we couldn't go. I bought this t-shirt with the tigers on it from our hotel. They had a shop that sold lots of things – clothes,

food, toys, even sports things.

F	Well, perhaps you can visit the zoo next time. Where else did you go?
Mch	We had a great day in the mountains when the weather was warm and sunny. We went really high. We didn't climb to the top but we walked up to the café and had lunch there. Look I bought this postcard there.
F	That's a lovely picture. You can put that on your wall. Was the weather always good?

A

B

C

D

E

F

G

H

Test 2, Listening Part 3   31

Mch Yes, but there was one day where it rained all day so we went to the museum. It was very interesting. I got this pen there. Do you like it?

F It's lovely! Did you visit anywhere else?

Mch Well, we went to a restaurant by the river on the last day. We had a big pizza and lots of ice cream. I got these chocolates from there. They make them at the restaurant. They're for you grandma!

R **Now listen to Part Three again.**

Answer Key ➤ SB page 30

Listening Part 4

In this part, students listen and tick the correct picture.

■ Warm-up

For suggested warm-up activities, see Test 1 page 14.

■ Do the test

Materials: SB pages 32 & 33, Audio T2P4

1 Ask students to turn to SB pages 32 & 33. Look at the five questions together and get students to think about what differences they can see in each set of pictures.

2 Play the recording and pause it after the example. Go through the example with the class, making sure they understand what they need to do.

3 Play the rest of the recording. As the students listen to the questions, they look at each set of pictures and tick the correct box, A, B or C.

4 Let students listen to the audio again. Check answers.

Audioscript

R **Listen and look. There is one example.**
Who is Robert going to go swimming with?

Mch Dad, can I go swimming this afternoon?

M I'm sorry Robert, but I have to go to the shops.

Mch That's OK. My friend Michael is going to go with his mum. I can go with them.

M Fine.

Mch Thanks Dad!

R **Can you see the tick? Now you listen and tick the box. One. What time must Robert come home?**

M What time are they going to go swimming?

Part 4
– 5 questions –

Listen and tick (✓) the box. There is one example.

Who is Robert going to go swimming with?

A ☐   B ✓   C ☐

1   What time must Robert come home?

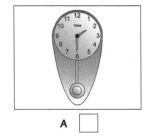 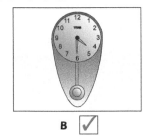 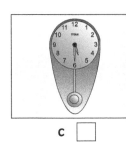

A ☐   B ✓   C ☐

2   How will Robert go to the swimming pool?

A ✓   B ☐   C ☐

32   Test 2, Listening Part 4

Mch At two thirty.

M OK, but you must come home at four thirty. Remember we're going to go to your grandma's for dinner and we need to leave at 5.30.

Mch OK, Dad.

R **Two. How will Robert go to the swimming pool?**

M Can Michael's mum take you in her car?

Mch She doesn't drive. They sometimes take the bus.

M How will you get to the swimming pool then? By bus?

Mch No, we'll ride our bikes there.

M That's a good idea.

R **Three. Where is Robert's swimming bag?**

Mch Do you know where my swimming bag is Dad?

M Isn't it in your bedroom?

Mch I've looked there. Is it in your car?

M It's not there. What about under the stairs?

Mch Oh yes, there it is!

R **Four. What is Robert going to have for lunch?**

M OK. I'll make some ham sandwiches for lunch.

3 Where is Robert's swimming bag?

 A ☐    B ☐    C ☑

4 What is Robert going to have for lunch?

 A ☑    B ☐   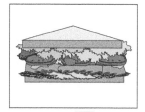 C ☐

5 What is Robert going to do before lunch?

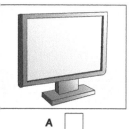 A ☐    B ☐    C ☑

Test 2, Listening Part 4   33

Mch Can we have pizza and chips?	**R** **Now listen to Part Four again.**
M Why don't we have a salad? It's not a good idea to have a big meal before swimming.	**Answer Key ➤** SB pages 32 & 33
Mch That's great!	
R **Five. What is Robert going to do before lunch?**	
M First I'd like you to clean your shoes.	
Mch I've already cleaned them – look! Can I watch some TV?	
M No, you can wash these plates for me.	
Mch All right, Dad.	

Listening Part 5

In this part, students listen and colour, draw and write on a picture.

■ Warm-up

For suggested warm-up activities, see Test 1 page 16.

■ Do the test

Materials: SB page 34, Audio T2P5, coloured pencils

1 Ask students to turn to SB page 34. Look at the picture with the class and ask them to name items and actions in the picture. Explain that they will listen to instructions in the form of a conversation between an adult and a child.

2 Play the recording and pause it after the example. Go through the example with the class. Make sure students understand that they will need to colour three things in the picture, write one word and draw one simple object (and also colour it).

3 Play the rest of the recording. The students listen and follow the instructions.

4 Let the students listen to the audio again. Check answers.

Audioscript

R **Listen and look at the picture.
There is one example.**

Fch I like that picture of a circus!

M Do you? Can you colour it for me then?

Fch Oh yes! Can I colour the man who's holding a monkey?

M OK. Can you colour his jacket?

Fch Yes, what colour?

M Red.

Part 5
– 5 questions –

Listen and colour and write and draw. There is one example.

Cold drinks & Ice cream

34 Test 2, Listening Part 5

R **Can you see the man's red jacket? This is an example. Now you listen and colour and write and draw.**

One

Fch What shall I colour now?

M Let's see. Can you see the women on the swings?

Fch Yes, I can.

M Well, look at the woman on the right. She's got long hair.

Fch Shall I colour her hair brown?

M OK.

R **Two**

Fch Shall I colour something else?

M I'd like you to write something now.

Fch OK.

M Now, can you see the man who's selling ice cream?

Fch Yes, I can! He's giving a little girl an ice cream.

M Well, can you write the word 'drinks' next to the word 'cold'? Do you see the space?

Fch Yes. There! I've done it!

R	**Three**
M	Now can you see the girl who's next to the boy with the balloon?
Fch	Yes, she's wearing a gold necklace.
M	That's right. Well I'd like you to draw a balloon in her hand.
Fch	All right and I'll colour it pink. Now they both have balloons!
M	Great.
R	**Four**
Fch	Shall I draw something else?
M	No, more colouring now. There's a woman who's standing next to the horse. Can you see her?
Fch	Yes.
M	Well, she's holding a fan. Can you colour it?
Fch	Yes. I'll do it green.
M	That's good.
R	**Five**
M	Last thing now. There are two clowns in the middle of the picture.
Fch	Yes, they're laughing at something.
M	Can you see the smaller one who's wearing a funny belt?
Fch	Yes, it's a very big belt.
M	I'd like you to colour it yellow.
Fch	OK. Is that all?
M	Yes. It's a lovely picture now.
R	**Now listen to Part Five again.**

Answer Key ➤ SB page 34

Reading & Writing
Part 1

In this part, students write the correct words next to the definitions.

■ Warm-up

For suggested warm-up activities, see Test 1 page 19.

■ Do the test

Materials: SB page 35

1 Ask students to turn to SB page 35. Look at the fifteen individual words and get students to think about what they mean.

2 Ask students to read through the ten definitions. Look at the example together.

3 Ask the students to match the definitions with the correct words. Remind them to copy the words carefully.

4 Check the answers.

Answer Key ➤ SB page 35

Part 1
– 10 questions –

Look and read. Choose the correct words and write them on the lines. There is one example.

maths   a hotel   wool   a rucksack

silver

soap

a brush

glue

This is a place where you can stay when you are on holiday.	a hotel
1 This is something we use to hold things together, for example, two pieces of paper.	glue
2 This is a bag you carry on your back.	a rucksack
3 You use this in the morning to make your hair look tidy.	a brush
4 You sleep in one of these outside when you go camping.	a tent
5 This school subject teaches you about things that happened in the past.	history
6 This is something we use when we wash our hands with water.	soap
7 These are places where people can study after they finish school.	universities
8 You can use this to help you see in the dark.	a torch
9 This is a school subject which teaches you about numbers.	maths
10 Gloves that we wear in winter are often made of this.	wool

a tent

a factory

a torch

universities

science   wood   history

Part 2
– 7 questions –

Look and read. Write yes or no.

Examples

A girl with long curly hair is throwing
a bottle in the bin.

yes

The big table at the café is round.

_no_

Reading & Writing
Part 2

In this part, students look at a
picture and then read sentences
and write yes or no answers.

■ Warm-up
For suggested warm-up
activities, see Test 1 page 20.

■ Do the test
Materials: SB pages 36 & 37

1 Ask students to turn to SB
pages 36 & 37. Look at the
picture together.

2 Ask students to look at the
two examples and discuss
these with the class. Ask them
to correct the second example,
e.g. _The big table at the café isn't
round._

3 The students now decide
whether the information in
the other seven sentences
about the picture are correct.
Remind students to write
either yes or _no_ after each
sentence.

Ask students to correct the
false sentences. (3 _The man
who's reading a newspaper hasn't
got a moustache. 5 The little girl
in the green dress has dropped
her doll. 7 The woman who is
getting on the train is carrying
a red handbag._)

Answer Key ➤ SB page 37

Questions

1   The woman who is sitting in the train is
    wearing sunglasses.   *yes*

2   The time on the clock in the railway station is
    quarter to one.   *yes*

3   The man who's reading a newspaper has got
    a moustache.   *no*

4   The little girl sitting on the suitcase is holding
    a blanket with spots on it.   *yes*

5   The little girl in the green dress has dropped
    her ball.   *no*

6   The taller boy who's waving is wearing
    a pair of green gloves.   *yes*

7   The woman who's getting on the train is carrying
    a red suitcase.   *no*

Part 3
– 5 questions –

Emma is talking to her friend, Helen. What does Helen say?

Read the conversation and choose the best answer.
Write a letter (A–H) for each answer.

You do not need to use all the letters.

Example

Emma:	What are you going to do this weekend?
Helen:	_____ D _____

Questions

1 Emma: Why are you going there?
  Helen: _____ C _____

2 Emma: Is it a new place?
  Helen: _____ A _____

3 Emma: What's the food like?
  Helen: _____ F _____

4 Emma: What time are you going?
  Helen: _____ H _____

5 Emma: So what have you bought your sister?
  Helen: _____ G _____

38 Test 2, Reading & Writing Part 3

Reading & Writing Part 3

In this part, students read a dialogue and select the correct response.

■ Warm-up
For suggested warm-up activities, see Test 1 page 22.

■ Do the test
Materials: SB pages 38 & 39

1 Ask students to turn to SB pages 38 & 39. Look at the gapped dialogue together and get students to think about what could go in the gaps.

2 Ask students to read the missing lines of the dialogue, options A–H.

3 Ask students to choose the appropriate line of dialogue from the options given and to write the correct letter in the space provided. Remind them that there is one extra line of dialogue that is not needed. Encourage students to read through the dialogue, quietly to themselves, to check that it makes sense.

4 Check answers.

Answer Key ➤ SB page 38

Test 2, Reading & Writing Part 3

Test 2

A	Yes. It opened last week.
B	Good – that's my favourite!
C	Because it's my sister's birthday.
D	We're going to go to a restaurant. **(Example)**
E	It's my birthday tomorrow.
F	The pizzas are great!
G	A bag. I hope she likes it.
H	About 8.00 p.m.

Part 4
– 6 questions –

Read the story. Choose a word from the box. Write the correct word next to numbers 1–5. There is one example.

Last Saturday, my dad took my brother and I to a campsite in the forest. We left

our _____*house*_____ after lunch. After a few hours we knew we were on the

wrong road because we couldn't see any **(1)** _____*trees*_____ ! We stopped

at a café and asked someone where the forest was. The man in the café

said, "You are three **(2)** _____*hours*_____ away from the forest!"

When we arrived at the campsite it was already **(3)** _____*dark*_____ , but my

dad had a torch in his car. We put the tent up and went to bed. In the middle of

the night it started to rain. It rained a lot and it was very windy. Suddenly the tent

fell down and water started to come **(4)** _____*into*_____ the tent. We were

very wet and we quickly ran to the car. The next morning we all woke up in the car

feeling **(5)** _____*tired*_____ and cold. We looked at our broken tent. "I don't

think we'll be sleeping in that tent again!" said my dad, and we all started to laugh.

Reading & Writing
Part 4

In this part, students choose and copy missing words from a story and then choose the best title.

■ Warm-up
For suggested warm-up activities, see Test 1 page 24.

■ Do the test
Materials: SB pages 40 & 41

1 Ask students to turn to SB pages 40 & 41. Look at the picture together and get students to think about the topic of the story.

2 Look at the example with the class and make sure they understand that they need to fill the gaps in the text from the words in the box. Remind students that there are more words than they need.

3 Ask students to fill in the five gaps in the story and to choose the best title for the story from the three options.

4 Check answers.

Answer Key ➤ SB pages 40 & 41

Example				
house	early	into	told	trees
caves	tired	outside	hours	dark

(6) Now choose the best name for the story.

Tick one box

The best campsite ☐

A Saturday to remember ☑

My favourite tent ☐

Part 5

– 7 questions –

Look at the picture and read the story. Write some words to complete the sentences about the story. You can use 1, 2, 3 or 4 words.

My dream day

My name's Lucy. My favourite singer is called Johnny B. He's very famous and when he was younger he was a student at our school. Our music teacher knows Johnny B and asked him to visit us. He said, "yes" and last Tuesday he came to our school.

I was very excited on that day and I couldn't wait to see Johnny B. I went into the music room with all the other students and sat down. Johnny B came into the room and talked to us about how he started singing and playing the guitar. Then he sang his new song, "Summer time". It was great!

After Johnny B left we went back to our classrooms for our afternoon lessons. While I was in my maths lesson, the music teacher came in and asked to see me and my friend Mary. My music teacher said that a journalist from our town's newspaper wanted to talk to some students about Johnny B's visit to our school. We couldn't believe it! We went to the school office where we answered some questions and the journalist took a photo of us. Yesterday my mum showed me our town newspaper. On the front page there was a picture of Johnny B and a picture of me and Mary! It was like a dream!

42   Test 2, Reading & Writing Part 5

Reading & Writing Part 5

In this part, students complete sentences about a story using one, two or three words.

■ Warm-up

For suggested warm-up activities, see Test 1 page 26.

■ Do the test

Materials: SB pages 42 & 43

1 Ask students to turn to SB pages 42 & 43. Look at the picture and get students to think about the topic of the story.

2 Ask students to read the story and then read the sentences. Then ask the students to underline the parts of the story that give them the information they need to complete the sentences.

3 Look at the example with the class and make sure they understand that they need to fill the gapped sentences using between one and four words. Remind the students that the words they will need to use will be in the story but may not be in the same order as the sentence.

4 Ask students to complete the gapped sentences.

5 Check the answers.

Answer Key ➤ SB page 43

Test 2

Examples

Johnny B is Lucy's _____favourite_____ singer.

Johnny B was a student at Lucy's school when _____he was younger_____ .

Questions

1   Lucy's music teacher asked Johnny B _____to visit_____ the school.

2   Lucy couldn't wait to see Johnny B and felt very _____excited_____ .

3   All the students sat in _____the music room_____ .

4   After he talked to the students, Johnny B sang _____his song_____ .

5   Lucy and Mary were in their _____classroom_____ when the music teacher asked to see them.

6   The journalist asked Lucy and Mary _____some questions_____ .

7   There was a photo of Lucy on the _____front page_____ of the newspaper.

Part 6
– 10 questions –

Read the text. Choose the right words and write them on the lines.

Airports

Example	Atlanta Airport is in the south east _____*of*_____ the
1	United States of America. Atlanta Airport _____*may*_____ not be
2	the biggest airport in the world, but it is the _____*busiest*_____ .
	More people fly in and out of Atlanta airport every year than any
3	other airport _____*in*_____ the world.
4	The airport is like _____*a*_____ small town. It has lots
5	of shops, cafés _____*and*_____ restaurants to choose from.
6	There is also a dog park for people _____*who*_____ are
	taking their pets on the plane with them. This is a park in the
7	airport where dogs can _____*run*_____ and play before
	they get on the plane.
8	_____*Lots*_____ of people who live in Atlanta work in the
9	airport. There _____*are*_____ many different kinds of jobs.
	Of course the airport needs pilots, but also waiters to work in the
10	cafés, doctors to help _____*any*_____ people who get ill
	and people to work in the many shops.

Reading & Writing
Part 6

In this part, students complete a text by selecting and copying the correct words.

■ Warm-up
For suggested warm-up activities, see Test 1 page 28.

■ Do the test
Materials: SB pages 44 & 45

1 Ask students to turn to SB pages 44 & 45. Look at the picture and get students to think about the topic of the text.
2 Go through the example.
3 Ask students to read the text and then read the word options.
4 Ask students to complete the gaps with a word.
5 Check the answers.

Answer Key ➤ SB page 44

Test 2

Example	of	to	for
1	should	may	will
2	busy	busier	busiest
3	from	in	on
4	a	an	the
5	but	so	and
6	how	who	what
7	run	runs	running
8	Many	Lots	Some
9	is	are	was
10	each	every	any

Part 7
– 5 questions –

Read the diary and write the missing words. Write one word on each line.

Saturday 14th September

Example I _____went_____ shopping with my mum this morning.

I bought some great new shoes. Mum made my favourite lunch

1 ___when / after___ we got home – sausages and chips! In

2 the afternoon Katy came _____to_____ my house.

3 We wanted to play on the computer, _____but_____

mum said we should play outside. Katy and I went to the

park and we met some friends from school. We sat and ate

4 ice cream. We _____had_____ a great time together!

5 We're going to go to the _____park_____ again tomorrow.

Reading & Writing Part 7

In this part, students complete a text with words of their own choice.

■ Warm-up
For suggested warm-up activities, see Test 1 page 30.

■ Do the test
Materials: SB page 46

1 Ask students to turn to SB page 46. Look at the gapped text together and get students to think about what sort of words are missing.

2 Look at the example together and ask students to identify whether it is a noun, verb, adjective, etc.

3 Ask students to complete each gap in the text with the missing word.

4 Check answers.

Answer Key ➤ SB page 46

Speaking Part 1

In this part, students identify and describe differences between two pictures.

■ Warm-up

For suggested warm-up activities, see Test 1 page 31.

■ Do the test

Materials: SB page 48, TB page 134

1 Ask the students some general introductory questions, e.g. *What's your surname? How old are you?*

2 Ask the students to turn to SB page 48. Give them time to look at the picture.

3 Turn to the Examiner's copy (TB page 134). Allow students to look at it briefly.

4 Make statements about your copy of the picture. Encourage the student to say how their picture is different. For example, *In my picture, the door is open. (In my picture, the door is closed.)*

Answer Key

1 girl playing violin / girl playing guitar

2 lizard on drum / star on drum

3 girl taking a photo / boy taking a photo

4 one girl drawing / both girls are reading

5 clock is next to picture / clock between pictures

6 boy playing piano is standing up / boy playing piano is sitting down

Candidate's copy

Part 1

Find the differences

48   Test 2, Speaking Part 1

Candidate's copy

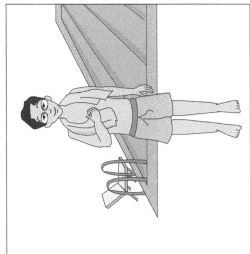

Information exchange

Ben's swimming club

What day	?
Time	?
Where	?
How long	?
Teacher	?

Sarah's tennis club

What day	Monday
Time	4:30 p.m.
Where	park
How long	2 hours
Teacher	Mr Drake

Test 2, Speaking Part 2   49

Speaking Part 2

In this part, students ask and answer questions using cues.

■ Warm-up

For suggested warm-up activities, see Test 1 page 32.

■ Do the test

Materials: SB page 49, TB page 135

1 Ask students to turn to SB page 49. Give them time to look at the pictures and the tables.

2 Look at the Examiner's copy (TB page 135). Ask the student questions about the information they have, e.g. *I don't know anything about Sarah's tennis club. What day is it on? (Monday)*.

3 Now encourage the student to ask you similar questions, e.g. *Where's Ben's swimming club?*

Answer Key ➤ Speaking frame page 59

Speaking Part 3

In this part, students continue a story by describing the pictures in sequence.

■ Warm-up

For suggested warm-up activities, see Test 1 page 33.

■ Do the test

Materials: SB page 50

1 Ask students to turn to SB page 50. Give them time to look at the pictures first.

2 Tell them the title and then describe the first picture, e.g.
These pictures tell a story.
It's called 'The kitten'. A boy has just opened his front door. etc.

3 Encourage the students to continue the story by describing the other pictures in turn. If necessary prompt them with a question.

Answer Key ➤ Speaking frame page 59

Speaking Part 4

In this part, students answer questions about themselves, their hobbies and their family or friends.

■ Warm-up

For suggested Warm-up activities, see Test 1 page 34.

■ Do the test

Materials: None

1 Ask the students several questions about themselves, their family or friends. They need only give simple answers, i.e. a phrase or a short sentence.
Now let's talk about your school.
What time do your lessons start?
How do you travel to school?
What is your favourite subject at school?
etc.

Part 3

Examiner's and Candidate's copy

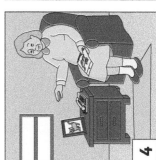

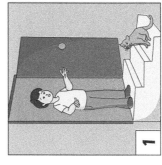

Tell the story

50　Test 2, Speaking Part 3

Speaking frame   (Timing = 7–9 minutes)

What to do	What to say	Answer from candidate	Back up question if necessary
	Hello ..., my name's ... *What's your surname?* *How old are you?*	*Hello* *(Fischer)* *(11)*	*What's your family name?* *Are you (11)?*
1 Show candidate both Find the differences pictures. Point to the girl playing the violin.	*Here are two pictures. My picture is nearly the same as yours, but some things are different.* *For example, in my picture the girl is playing a violin, but in your picture she's playing guitar.* *I'm going to say something about my picture. You tell me how your picture is different.* *In my picture, there is a lizard on the big drum.* *In my picture, a girl is taking a photo.* *In my picture, one girl on the floor is drawing.* *In my picture, the clock is next to a picture.* *In my picture, the door is open.* *In my picture, the boy playing the piano is standing up.*	*In my picture, there is a star on the big drum.* *In my picture, a boy is taking a photo.* *In my picture, the girls on the floor are reading.* *In my picture, the clock is between two pictures.* *In my picture, the door is closed.* *In my picture, the boy playing the piano is sitting down.*	*Point to the other differences which the student does not mention.* *Is there a picture of a lizard on the drum?* *Is it a girl who is taking a photo?* *Are the girls on the floor drawing?* *Is the clock below two pictures?* *Is the door open?* *Is the boy playing the piano standing up?*
2 Point to both candidate's and examiner's copies. Point to the picture of the girl before asking the questions. Point to the picture of the boy.	*Sarah and Ben both go to clubs after school. I don't know anything about Sarah's tennis club, but you do. So I'm going to ask you some questions.* *What day does Sarah go to tennis club?* *What time does it start?* *Where is her tennis club?* *How long is her tennis club?* *What is her teacher called?* *Now you don't know anything about Ben's swimming club, so you ask me some questions.* *(Friday)* *(5:15 p.m.)* *(at the sports centre)* *(1 hour)* *(Mrs Crewe)*	*Monday* *4:30 p.m.* *In the park* *2 hours* *Mr Drake* *What day does Ben go to swimming club?* *What time does it start?* *Where is his swimming club?* *How long is his swimming club?* *What is his teacher called?*	*Point to the information if necessary.* *Point to the information if necessary.*
3 Point to the picture story. Allow time to look at the pictures.	*These pictures tell a story.* *It's called 'The kitten'. Just look at the pictures first.* *A boy has just opened his front door. There is a kitten sitting outside the front door. The boy looks surprised to see the kitten. He doesn't know where the kitten has come from.* *Now you tell the story.*	*2 – The boy has taken the kitten inside his house. He is giving the kitten some milk and some food. The kitten looks happy now.* *3 – The boy has put a picture of the kitten on a tree. There is a telephone number on the picture.* *4 – An old lady is holding the picture of the kitten. She is phoning the number on the picture. It is her kitten because she has a photo of it on her table.* *5 – The boy has given the kitten back to the old woman. The woman and the kitten look very happy. The boy looks surprised and happy because the old woman has given him a present.*	*Where is the kitten now?* *What is the boy giving the kitten?* *What is the boy putting on the tree?* *What information is on the picture of the kitten?* *What is the old woman holding?* *What is she doing?* *What is on her table?* *What has the boy done?* *How does the old woman feel?* *Why is the boy looking surprised and happy?*
4 Put away all pictures. Ask a few personal questions.	*Now let's talk about your school.* *What time do your lessons start at school?* *How do you travel to school?* *What is your favourite subject at school?* *How many children are there in your class?* *Tell me about what you usually do after school.* *OK, thank you (name).* *Goodbye.*	*Quarter to nine* *By bus* *Maths* *30* *I like to play with my friends. We usually play computer games. I have dinner with my family.* *Goodbye.*	*Do your lessons start at nine o'clock?* *Do you travel to school by bus?* *What school subject do you like the best?* *Are there 30 children in your class?* *Do you like to play with your friends after school?* *What do you like to do with your friends?* *Do you eat dinner with your family?*

Test 3

Listening Part 1

In this part, students listen and draw lines to match names to people in a picture.

■ Warm-up

For suggested warm-up activities, see Test 1 page 8.

■ Do the test

Materials: SB page 52, Audio T3P1

1 Ask students to turn to SB page 52. Look at the picture together and get students to read the names.

2 Play the recording and pause it after the example. Go through the example with the class.

3 Play the rest of the recording. The students draw a line from the names to the appropriate people in the picture.

4 Let the students listen to the audio again. Check answers.

Audioscript

R	**Listen and look. There is One example.**
Mch	I went camping last weekend. Do you want to have a look at my photo?
F	Yes, please. Did you enjoy it?
Mch	Yes, we had a great time. Can you see the boy who's playing the guitar?
F	Which one? The one with blonde hair?
Mch	Yes. He's called William. We met him there.
R	**Can you see the line? This is an example. Now you listen and draw lines.**
F	Who's that girl who's sitting in the tent?
Mch	There are two tents. Which one do you mean?
F	The bigger green tent.
Mch	The girl who's wearing a scarf?
F	Yes, she looks a bit cold.
Mch	Oh, that's Daisy. I think she felt cold all weekend!

Now the right-hand portion:

F	Look at those boys who are cooking on the fire!
Mch	Yes, the boy who's cooking sausages is my brother, Nick. The other boy's his friend from school.
F	The food looks good!
Mch	Yes, it was.
F	Who are those two women?
Mch	The ones who're standing next to the tent?
F	No, the ones who're sitting on chairs next to the tree.
Mch	Oh, those women! The one with the yellow jacket's my mum and the other woman's her friend, Jill.
F	Did your dad go with you?
Mch	No, he worked all weekend.
F	So who's the man in the car?
Mch	That's my mum and dad's friend, John. He drove us there.
F	Where's your friend Emma?
Mch	Oh, she's taking her rucksack out of the car.
F	Is that her with the blue one?
Mch	No, hers is orange – it's very heavy.
F	Yes, she looks unhappy!
R	**Now listen to Part One again.**

Answer Key ➤ SB page 52

Part 1
– 5 questions –

Listen and draw lines. There is one example.

Daisy   William   Nick   Emma

Helen   Jill   John

52   Test 3, Listening Part 1

Part 2
– 5 questions –

Listen and write. There is one example.

HOMEWORK: JOB INFORMATION

Surname:		Mr _____ *White*
1	**Job:**	*cook*
2	**Works in:**	*hospital*
3	**Age when started job:**	*21 / twenty-one*
4	**Where learnt job:**	*college*
5	**Colour of uniform:**	white and ____ *grey*

Test 3, Listening Part 2   53

Listening Part 2
In this part, students listen and write words or numbers in gaps.

■ Warm-up
For suggested warm-up activities see Test 1 page 10.

■ Do the test
Materials: SB page 53, Audio T3P2

1 Ask students to turn to SB page 53. Look at the form together and get students to think about what kind of information is missing.

2 Play the recording and pause it after the example. Go through the example with the class.

3 Play the rest of the recording. The students listen and fill in the missing words on the form.

4 Let the students listen to the audio again. Check answers.

Audioscript
R   **Listen and look. There is one example.**

Fch Can I ask you some questions, Mr White?

M   Yes, of course, Jane. What do you want to know?

Fch Well it's for my school homework. I have to find out information about someone's job.

M   Oh, OK.

Fch How do you spell your surname?

M   It's W-H-I-T-E.

Fch Thank you.

R   **Can you see the answer? Now you listen and write.**

Fch What's your job, Mr White?

M   I'm a cook.

Fch Oh, that's an unusual job.

M   Well ... I love food.

Fch Me too!
So do you work in a restaurant?

M   No, I've never worked in one of those. I work in a hospital. I cook the food for all the people who are ill and for the doctors and nurses who work there.

Fch Wow! That's a lot of people.

M   Yes. I'm always busy.

Fch How old were you when you started your job?

M   I was much younger than I am now! I was twenty-one. I remember because I started the job the day after my birthday.

Fch And where did you learn how to do your job? Did you go to university?

M   I didn't need to do that. I went to college and learned everything there. I wasn't a very good student!

Fch Right. And the last question, do you wear a uniform at work?

M   Yes. Everyone who works in the kitchens has to wear a uniform. It's white and grey. I like the uniform, but it's difficult to keep clean!

Fch Yes, I'm sure! Thank you for answering my questions, Mr White.

M   You're welcome! I'm happy to help.

R   **Now listen to Part Two again.**

Answer Key ➤ SB page 53

Listening Part 3

In this part, students listen and match pictures to words or names by writing a letter in the box.

■ Warm-up

For suggested warm-up activities, see Test 1 page 12.

■ Do the test

Materials: SB pages 54 & 55, Audio T3P3

1 Ask students to turn to SB pages 54 & 55. Look at the list of illustrated names and the set of pictures with the class.

2 Play the recording and pause it after the example. Go through the example with the class, making sure they understand what they need to do.

3 Play the rest of the recording. The students listen and match the illustrated names with the pictures, A to H.

4 Let the students listen to the audio again. Check answers.

Audioscript

R	**Listen and look. There is one example. What sports do Anna's friends do?**
M	Why don't you start a new sport Anna? You spend too much time in your bedroom. What sports do your friends do?
Fch	Well, Bill loves volleyball. He plays it at the beach at the weekend. I've tried it too but I'm not very good.
R	**Can you see the letter 'G'? Now you listen and write a letter in each box.**
M	What about your best friend, does she do any sport?
Fch	You mean Sue. She's good at running. She runs with her dad every morning before school. But I don't

Part 3
– 5 questions –

What sports do Anna's friends do?

Listen and write a letter in each box. There is one example.

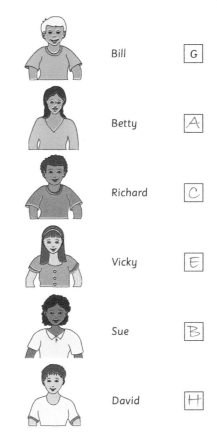

Bill G

Betty A

Richard C

Vicky E

Sue B

David H

think I have time before school, and I don't like running races.

M	Well who else is there?
Fch	Do you remember my friend David? He's the boy I had guitar lessons with. He plays golf. He goes to the club next to the park. We could do that together at the weekends.
M	That's a good idea. Or how about tennis?
Fch	Yes, I could play tennis with Vicky. No, sorry, she stopped playing tennis last year. Now she plays

badminton. She loves it and she's won lots of competitions.

M	I liked that sport when I was young – but I didn't win any competitions! What about your other friends?
Fch	Betty plays hockey for the school team – she's very good. She started playing 3 years ago when she was only eight. We play it at school sometimes too, but I don't like it very much.
M	Does anyone play baseball?

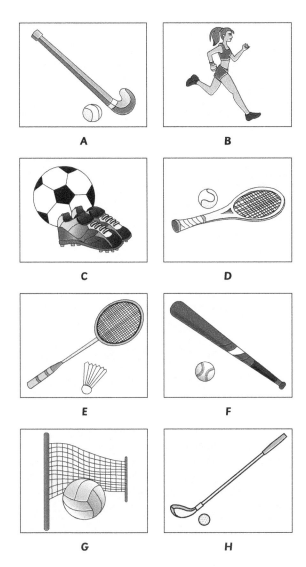

Fch Richard played baseball a lot when he lived in America, but he says it's difficult to find people who play it here. He plays football now and he goes to the school club. They have a club for girls too. Perhaps I could try that. I'll ask the sports teacher at school tomorrow.

M Well, that sounds like a good idea.

R **Now listen to Part Three again.**

Answer Key ➤ SB page 54

Listening Part 4

In this part, students listen and tick the correct picture.

■ Warm-up

For suggested warm-up activities, see Test 1 page 14.

■ Do the test

Materials: SB pages 56 & 57, Audio T3P4

1 Ask students to turn to SB pages 56 & 57. Look at the five questions together and get students to think about what differences they can see in each set of pictures.

2 Play the recording and pause it after the example. Go through the example with the class, making sure they understand what they need to do.

3 Play the rest of the recording. As the students listen to the questions, they look at each set of pictures and tick the correct box, A, B or C.

4 Let students listen to the audio again. Check answers.

Audioscript

R **Listen and look. There is one example. Where is Michael going to go with his school class?**

F Are you going to go to the forest with your school class next week, Michael?

Mch No, we wanted to go to the river grandma, but we're going to stay in the mountains this time.

F That sounds fun.

Mch Yes, I can't wait!

R **Can you see the tick? Now you listen and tick the box.**
One. Where is Michael going to stay?

F Where are you going to stay?

Part 4
– 5 questions –

Listen and tick (✓) the box. There is one example.

Where is Michael going to go with his school class?

A ☐   B ☐   C ✓

1   Where is Michael going to stay?

  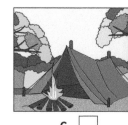

A ✓   B ☐   C ☐

2   What is the weather going to be like?

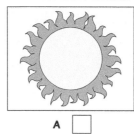 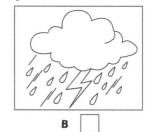 

A ☐   B ☐   C ✓

56   Test 3, Listening Part 4

Mch Well, the hotels are too expensive.

F Are you going to camp then?

Mch No, we're going to stay on a farm. I think it'll be lots of fun!

R **Two. What is the weather going to be like?**

F I hope the weather's going to be warm and sunny.

Mch No, I think it's going to be cloudy and windy, but not very cold.

F Well that's better than rain.

Mch Yes.

R **Three. Which backpack is Michael going to take?**

F So have you got everything you need?

Mch I do now, but I couldn't find my blue backpack with the red pocket and I didn't want to use my sister's. It's got spots on it!

F I see.

Mch Mum bought me a new one with a footballer on it – I love it!

R **Four. When is Michael going to visit his grandma?**

Which backpack is Michael going to take?

 A ☐

 B ✓

 C ☐

When is Michael going to visit his grandma?

 A ☐

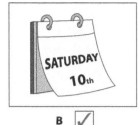 B ✓

 C ☐

What is Michael going to eat at his grandma's house?

 A ✓

 B ☐

 C ☐

Test 3, Listening Part 4 57

F	Are you going to visit me after your holiday?
Mch	Yes, grandma. We'll get back on Friday.
F	Would you like to come for lunch on Sunday?
Mch	Sorry, I'm going to play football that day. What about Saturday?
F	That's fine.
R	**Five. What is Michael going to eat at his grandma's house?**
F	I'll cook your favourite meal … fish and chips!
Mch	Thanks grandma, but that's my sister's favourite. I prefer pizza.
F	Oh yes, sorry! OK, and I'll get some sausages for your dad.
Mch	See you then!
R	**Now listen to Part Four again.**

Answer Key ➤ SB pages 56 & 57

Listening Part 5

In this part, students listen and colour, draw and write on a picture.

■ Warm-up

For suggested warm-up activities, see Test 1 page 16.

■ Do the test

Materials: SB page 58, Audio T3P5, coloured pencils

1 Ask students to turn to SB page 58. Look at the picture with the class and ask them to name items and actions in the picture. Explain that they will listen to instructions in the form of a conversation between an adult and a child.

2 Play the recording and pause it after the example. Go through the example with the class. Make sure students understand that they will need to colour three things in the picture, write one word and draw one simple object (and also colour it).

3 Play the rest of the recording. The pupils listen and follow the instructions.

4 Let the students listen to the audio again. Check answers.

Audioscript

R   **Listen and look at the picture. There is one example.**

F   This is a picture of the dentist's where I work. Do you want to colour it?

Mch   Yes, please.

F   Can you see the little boy who's looking at the fish?

Mch   Yes, he's standing next to a little girl.

F   That's right. Can you colour his trousers green?

Mch   OK.

Part 5
– 5 questions –

Listen and colour and write and draw. There is one example.

R   **Can you see the boy's green trousers? This is an example. Now you listen and colour and write and draw.**
One

F   Good. Now then, the boy and girl are looking at three fish.

Mch   Yes, there's a big fish and two smaller ones.

F   That's right. Do you want to colour the big fish with the stripes?

Mch   OK, what colour?

F   Oh, I don't know ... red?

Mch   Yes, that's a good colour.

R   **Two**

F   Now, can you see the lady who's working on the computer?

Mch   Yes, she's talking to an old man.

F   That's right. She's wearing glasses and has got long hair.

Mch   Yes. She looks very friendly. Can I colour her hair brown?

F   No. Colour it pink!

Mch   All right! I've done it!

R	**Three**
F	Now I'd like you to do some writing.
Mch	OK.
F	Can you see the picture on the wall to the right of the door?
Mch	Yes, there's a bowl and a spoon.
F	That's right. Write the word 'sugar' under 'No'.
Mch	There ..... That's it!

R	**Four**
F	Good. Can you see the coffee table which has some magazines on it?
Mch	Yes, there are two biscuits on it.
F	Yes. I'd like you to draw another biscuit.
Mch	OK. Where shall I draw it?
F	You can draw it in the space between the two other biscuits.
Mch	OK and I'll colour it orange.

R	**Five**
F	Right. Now I'd like you to colour something.
Mch	Oh good. Shall I colour the table?
F	Not now. Can you see the three pictures on the wall?
Mch	The pictures of butterflies?
F	Yes. I'd like you to colour the butterfly with the spots.
Mch	OK. Shall I colour it purple?
F	That's a good idea. It looks very nice!
Mch	Thanks!

R	**Now listen to Part Five again.**

Answer Key ➤ SB page 58

Reading & Writing
Part 1

In this part, students write the correct words next to the definitions.

■ Warm-up

For suggested warm-up activities, see Test 1 page 19.

■ Do the test

Materials: SB page 59

1 Ask students to turn to SB page 59. Look at the fifteen individual words and get students to think about what they mean.

2 Ask students to read through the ten definitions. Look at the example together.

3 Ask the students to match the definitions with the correct words. Remind them to copy the words carefully.

4 Check the answers.

Answer Key ➤ SB page 59

Part 1
– 10 questions –

Look and read. Choose the correct words and write them on the lines. There is one example.

autumn   a shelf   a camel   fog

a storm   a swan   ice   magazines

a key   a swing   summer   a butterfly

This is a season. The weather is usually warm and sunny. — *summer*

1 This is something you usually find on a wall. We can put books on it. — *a shelf*

2 This is a large white bird with a long neck. You often see it on rivers or lakes. — *a swan*

3 This is cloud just above the ground which makes it difficult to see. — *fog*

4 This is very bad weather when there is a lot of wind, rain or snow. — *a storm*

5 This is the part of the year that comes before winter. — *autumn*

6 This is an insect with large wings. They can be many different colors. — *a butterfly*

7 You need this to buy things in shops. — *money*

8 This is made of metal and you can use it to open doors. — *a key*

9 People often read these to find out about their favorite singers or actors. — *magazines*

10 This animal can carry heavy things and can walk for a long time without water. — *a camel*

a sofa   money   week

Part 2
– 7 questions –

Look and read. Write yes or no.

Examples

It's sunny outside and the sky is blue. _____yes_____

The cupboard doors are both closed. _____no_____

Reading & Writing
Part 2

In this part, students look at a picture and then read sentences and write *yes* or *no* answers.

■ Warm-up
For suggested warm-up activities, see Test 1 page 20.

■ Do the test
Materials: SB pages 60 & 61

1 Ask students to turn to SB pages 60 & 61. Look at the picture together.

2 Ask students to look at the two examples and discuss these with the class. Ask them to correct the second example, e.g. *One cupboard door is open.*

3 The students now decide whether the information in the other seven sentences about the picture are correct. Remind students to write either *yes* or *no* after each sentence. Ask students to correct the false sentences. (3 *The girl who's studying at the table isn't listening to music.* 4 *The man who's cleaning the window hasn't got a moustache.* 6 *The boy who is standing next to the old woman is holding two books.*)

Answer Key ➤ SB page 61

Questions

1   The baby boy has pulled some books out of the bookcase.   _yes_

2   The man who's wearing glasses looks very angry.   _yes_

3   The girl who's studying at the table is also listening to music.   _no_

4   The man who's cleaning the window has got a moustache.   _no_

5   The old woman is wearing a skirt which is purple and black.   _yes_

6   A boy is standing next to the old woman and he's holding more than four books.   _no_

7   The yellow books are bigger than the books that are on the floor.   _yes_

Part 3
– 5 questions –

Robert is talking to his friend, Harry. What does Harry say?

Read the conversation and choose the best answer.
Write a letter (A–H) for each answer.

You do not need to use all the letters.

Example

	Robert:	Did you see that TV programme about the most dangerous animals in the world?
	Harry:	E

Questions

1   **Robert:**   Did you like it?

       Harry: H

2   **Robert:**   Did you see the part about the octopus?

       Harry: G

3   **Robert:**   Which part did you like best?

       Harry: D

4   **Robert:**   Did you see the man who swam with sharks?

       Harry: A

5   **Robert:**   I'd like to swim with dolphins.

       Harry: C

Reading & Writing
Part 3

In this part, students read a dialogue and select the correct response.

■ Warm-up
For suggested warm-up activities, see Test 1 page 22

■ Do the test
Materials: SB pages 62 & 63

1 Ask students to turn to SB pages 62 & 63. Look at the gapped dialogue together and get students to think about what could go in the gaps.

2 Ask students to read the missing lines of the dialogue, options A–H.

3 Ask students to choose the appropriate line of dialogue from the options given and to write the correct letter in the space provided. Remind them that there is one extra line of dialogue that is not needed. Encourage students to read through the dialogue, quietly to themselves, to check that it makes sense.

4 Check answers.

Answer Key ➤ SB page 62

Test 3

A	Yes, he was very brave.
B	Whales are bigger than sharks.
C	Yes, I'd like that too!
D	I don't know. It's difficult to choose.
E	Yes, I did. **(Example)**
F	That's wonderful!
G	No, I hate them so I didn't watch that part.
H	Oh, yes. It was great.

Part 4
– 6 questions –

Read the story. Choose a word from the box. Write the correct word next to numbers 1–5. There is one example.

My name's Tom and I have a dog _____*called*_____ Buster. One day last

summer I was watching TV in my house **(1)** _____*when*_____ Buster ran into

the living room. I knew that something was wrong because Buster was jumping up

and down and **(2)** _____*making*_____ a lot of noise. When I asked Buster, "What

is wrong?", he started running to the front door. I followed him outside. He wanted

to get out of our garden so I followed him into the **(3)** _____*street*_____ .

He stood in front of the house next to ours. Buster started making a lot of

noise again. Then I saw what the problem was. I could see a **(4)** _____*fire*_____

through the kitchen window. I ran back home and called my mum. My mum phoned

for help and a fire engine soon arrived. The old woman who lives in the house wasn't

hurt. She was **(5)** _____*upstairs*_____ when the firemen arrived.

That night I gave Buster a big bowl of his favourite food!

Reading & Writing
Part 4

In this part, students choose and copy missing words from a story and then choose the best title.

■ Warm-up

For suggested warm-up activities, see Test 1 page 24.

■ Do the test

Materials: SB pages 64 & 65

1 Ask students to turn to SB pages 64 & 65. Look at the picture together and get students to think about the topic of the story.

2 Look at the example with the class and make sure they understand that they need to fill the gaps in the text from the words in the box. Remind students that there are more words than they need.

3 Ask students to fill in the five gaps in the story and to choose the best title for the story from the three options.

4 Check answers.

Answer Key ➤ SB pages 64 & 65

Test 3

Example				
called	street	making	quickly	upstairs
when	opened	wood	fire	said

(6) Now choose the best name for the story.

Tick one box

An exciting summer ☐

The old lady and the terrible fire ☐

My clever dog ☑

Part 5

– 7 questions –

Look at the picture and read the story. Write some words to complete the sentences about the story. You can use 1, 2, 3 or 4 words.

The wrong suitcase

Last month, Harry went on holiday with his mum and dad. They went to a cheap hotel by the sea for a week. Harry was very happy because they were travelling by plane. It was Harry's first time in a plane. When they arrived at the airport, Harry and his parents went to get their suitcases. His parents had a big red suitcase and Harry had a small one with black stripes.

Then they took a taxi to their hotel. Harry thought the hotel was excellent because it had a very big swimming pool. Harry wanted to go for a swim before he did anything else. He went to his room and opened his suitcase to get his swimming shorts. Harry was very surprised when he opened his suitcase. It was full of dresses! It wasn't Harry's suitcase! His mum found a name and phone number in the suitcase and she called the number. The woman on the phone said she had Harry's suitcase.

That afternoon Harry and his parents met the woman. She was very happy to get her suitcase back and she wanted to thank them. The woman was very rich and the next day Harry and his parents had lunch with her – on her boat! It was Harry's best holiday!

Reading & Writing
Part 5

In this part, students complete sentences about a story using one, two or three words.

■ Warm-up

For suggested warm-up activities, see Test 1 page 26.

■ Do the test

Materials: SB pages 66 & 67

1 Ask students to turn to SB pages 66 & 67. Look at the picture and get students to think about the topic of the story.

2 Ask students to read the story and then read the sentences. Then ask the students to underline the parts of the story that give them the information they need to complete the sentences.

3 Look at the example with the class and make sure they understand that they need to fill the gapped sentences using between one and four words. Remind the students that the words they will need to use will be in the story but may not be in the same order as the sentence.

4 Ask students to complete the gapped sentences.

5 Check the answers.

Answer Key ➤ SB page 67

Test 3

Examples

Harry and his parents went on holiday last _____ month _____ .

Their hotel, which was next to _____ the sea _____ , was cheap.

Questions

1 Harry felt _____ happy _____ about travelling by plane.

2 Harry and his parents got their suitcases when _____ they arrived _____
   at the airport.

3 Harry's suitcase was small and had _____ black stripes _____ .

4 They travelled to the hotel by _____ taxi _____ .

5 Harry liked the hotel because it had a _____ swimming pool _____ .

6 Harry found _____ dresses _____ in his suitcase.

7 Harry and his parents had _____ lunch _____ on the woman's boat.

Part 6
– 10 questions –

Read the text. Choose the right words and write them on the lines.

Mount Everest

Example	Mount Everest is ____the____ highest mountain in the
1	world. The mountain is ____between____ two countries,
2	Nepal and China. Every year many men ____and____
3	women try to climb Mount Everest. It is not ____easy____
	to climb a big mountain and many people don't get to the top.
4	It snows a lot ____on____ Mount Everest and so you
	need to wear warm clothes like socks and gloves made of wool.
5	There ____are____ no roads or cars on the way up the
6	mountain so people need to carry ____everything____ . Some
	people use animals called 'Yaks' to help them carry things. Yaks are
7	like cows and have ____lots____ of fur. Their fur helps
	them keep warm in the snow.
8	People ____who____ climb the mountain need to take a tent
	with them because they will need to somewhere to sleep at night.
9	____They____ also need to carry food in their rucksacks.
10	It ____takes____ many days to climb Mount Everest.

Reading & Writing Part 6

In this part, students complete a text by selecting and copying the correct words.

■ Warm-up
For suggested warm-up activities, see Test 1 page 28.

■ Do the test
Materials: SB pages 68 & 69

1 Ask students to turn to SB pages 68 & 69. Look at the picture and get students to think about the topic of the text.
2 Go through the example.
3 Ask students to read the text and then read the word options.
4 Ask students to complete the gaps with a word.
5 Check the answers.

Answer Key ➤ SB page 68

Example	a	the	an
1	between	under	behind
2	but	and	so
3	easy	easier	easiest
4	to	on	of
5	are	is	were
6	everywhere	everyone	everything
7	lots	many	much
8	what	who	which
9	They	Them	Their
10	take	taking	takes

Part 7
– 5 questions –

Read the letter and write the missing words. Write one word on each line.

	Dear Jane,
Example	How _____*are*_____ you? I can't wait for you to come
	and visit next weekend. My mum is going to take us to
1	the zoo _____*on*_____ Saturday. My brother's been
	there before and he says it's great! On Saturday night we
2	can go _____*to*_____ the cinema. There's a funny
3	film that I think _____*you*_____ will like. On Sunday
4	we can _____*play*_____ golf in the park.
5	The _____*weather*_____ is very hot and sunny here so bring
	your summer clothes!
	See you soon,
	Alex

Reading & Writing
Part 7

In this part, students complete a text with words of their own choice.

■ Warm-up

For suggested warm-up activities, see Test 1 page 30.

■ Do the test

Materials: SB page 70

1 Ask students to turn to SB page 70. Look at the gapped text together and get students to think about what sort of words are missing.

2 Look at the example together and ask students to identify whether it is a noun, verb, adjective, etc.

3 Ask students to complete each gap in the text with the missing word.

4 Check answers.

Answer Key ➤ SB page 70

Test 3

Speaking Part 1

In this part, students identify and describe differences between two pictures.

■ Warm-up

For suggested warm-up activities, see Test 1 page 31.

■ Do the test

Materials: SB page 72, TB page 136

1 Ask the students some general introductory questions, e.g. *What's your surname? How old are you?*

2 Ask the students to turn to SB page 72. Give them time to look at the picture.

3 Turn to the Examiner's copy (TB page 136). Allow students to look at it briefly.

4 Make statements about your copy of the picture. Encourage the student to say how their picture is different. For example, *In my picture, there are two horses. (In my picture, there are three.)*

Answer Key

1 tree next to farmer / no tree

2 the boy is holding a toy cat / boy holding toy chicken

3 there are five cows / four cows

4 puppy is drinking water / dog is drinking water

5 frogs are sitting on bigger rock / frogs are on smaller rock

6 farmer wearing a black hat / farmer wearing a brown hat

7 one duck / two ducks in the water

Candidate's copy

Part 1

Find the differences

72 Test 3, Speaking Part 1

Candidate's copy

Information exchange

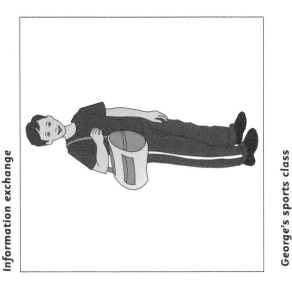

Katy's sports class

Teacher's name	?
What day	?
What time / start	?
How many children	?
What sport / learn	?

George's sports class

Teacher's name	Mr Butt
What day	Tuesday
What time / start	2:15
How many children	25
What sport / learn	hockey

Test 3, Speaking Part 2   73

Speaking Part 2

In this part, students ask and answer questions using cues.

■ Warm-up

For suggested warm-up activities, see Test 1 page 32

■ Do the test

Materials: SB page 73, TB page 137

1 Ask students to turn to SB page 73. Give them time to look at the pictures and the tables.

2 Look at the Examiner's copy (TB page 137). Ask the student questions about the information they have, e.g. *I don't know anything about George's sports class. What's the teacher's name? (Mr Butt).*

3 Now encourage the student to ask you similar questions, e.g. *What day is Katy's sports class on?*

Answer Key ➤ Speaking frame page 83

Speaking Part 3

In this part, students continue a story by describing the pictures in sequence.

■ Warm-up

For suggested warm-up activities, see Test 1 page 33.

■ Do the test

Materials: SB page 74

1 Ask students to turn to SB page 74. Give them time to look at the pictures first.

2 Tell them the title and then describe the first picture, e.g. *These pictures tell a story. It's called 'The birthday'. A woman is having breakfast.* etc.

3 Encourage the students to continue the story by describing the other pictures in turn. If necessary prompt them with a question.

Answer Key ➤ Speaking frame page 83

Speaking Part 4

In this part, students answer questions about themselves, their hobbies and their family or friends.

■ Warm-up

For suggested Warm-up activities, see Test 1 page 34.

■ Do the test

Materials: None

1 Ask the students several questions about themselves, their family or friends. They need only give simple answers, i.e. a phrase or a short sentence.
Now let's talk about food.
What is your favourite food?
Who does most of the cooking at home?
What time do you usually eat dinner?
etc.

Examiner's and Candidate's copy

Part 3

Tell the story

74 Test 3, Speaking Part 3

Speaking frame   (Timing = 5–7 minutes)

What to do	What to say	Answer from candidate	Back up question if necessary
	Hello..., my name's ... What's your surname? How old are you?	Hello (Fischer) (11)	What's your family name? Are you (11)?
1 Show candidate both Find the Differences pictures. Point to the lake in each picture, showing that in one picture there is a tree, but in the picture there isn't.	Here are two pictures. My picture is nearly the same as yours, but some things are different. For example, in my picture there is a tree next to the farmer, but in your picture there isn't. I'm going to say something about my picture. You tell me how your picture is different. In my picture, there are two horses. In my picture, the boy is holding a toy cat. In my picture, there are five cows. In my picture, the puppy is drinking water from a bowl. In my picture, the frogs are sitting on the bigger rock. In my picture, the farmer is wearing a black hat.	In my picture, there are three horses. In my picture, the boy is holding a toy chicken. In my picture, there are four cows. In my picture, the dog is drinking water from a bowl. In my picture, the frogs are sitting on the smaller rock. In my picture, the farmer is wearing a brown hat.	Point to the other differences which the student does not mention. Are there two horses? Is the boy holding a toy cat? Are there five cows? Is the puppy drinking water from a bowl? Are the frogs sitting on the bigger rock? Is the farmer wearing a black hat?
2 Point to both candidate's and examiner's copies. Point to the picture of the boy before asking the questions. Point to the picture of the girl.	George and Katy both have sports lessons at school. I don't know anything about George's sports class, but you do. So I'm going to ask you some questions. What is David's sports teacher called? What day is David's sports lesson? What time does the lesson start? How many children are in David's class? What sport is David's class learning to play? Now you don't know anything about Katy's sports class, so you ask me some questions. (Miss Keen) (Friday) (1:45) (28) (Volleyball)	Mr Butt Tuesday 2:15 25 Hockey What is Katy's sports teacher called? What day is Katy's sports lesson? What time does the lesson start? How many children are in Katy's class? What sport is Katy's class learning to play?	Point to the information if necessary. Point to the information if necessary.
3 Point to the picture story. Allow time to look at the pictures.	These pictures tell a story. It's called 'The birthday'. Just look at the pictures first. A woman is having breakfast with her family. She looks sad because she thinks her family has forgotten her birthday. Now you tell the story.	2 – The man and children are waving goodbye to the woman. The woman is going to work. She still looks unhappy. 3 – The man and the children have made a cake. The man is taking the cake out of the cooker. 4 – The man and the children are getting the room ready for the birthday party. The man is putting cups on the table and the children are putting presents on the table. 5 – The woman has come home from work. She has just opened the door. She looks very happy and very surprised. There are lots of people at the party.	What are the man and the children doing? Where is the woman going? What have the man and the children made? What is the man doing? What are the children doing? What has the woman just done? How does the woman feel? Are there any other people at the party?
4 Put away all pictures. Ask a few personal questions.	Now let's talk about food. What is your favourite food? Who does most of the cooking at home? What time do you usually eat dinner? Where in your house do you usually eat meals? Tell me about your favourite place to eat. OK, thank you (name). Goodbye.	Pizza My mum At 6 o'clock In our kitchen My favourite restaurant is Mario's. I usually eat pasta. We go there for my birthday. Goodbye.	Is pizza your favourite food? Does your mum do most of the cooking? Do you usually eat dinner at 6 o'clock? Do you usually eat your meals in the kitchen? Do you have a favourite restaurant or café? What do you like to eat there? When do you eat there?

Test 4

Listening Part 1

In this part, students listen and draw lines to match names to people in a picture.

■ Warm-up

For suggested warm-up activities, see Test 1 page 8.

■ Do the test

Materials: SB page 76, Audio T4P1

1 Ask students to turn to SB page 76. Look at the picture together and get students to read the names.

2 Play the recording and pause it after the example. Go through the example with the class.

3 Play the rest of the recording. The students draw a line from the names to the appropriate people in the picture.

4 Let the students listen to the audio again. Check answers.

Audioscript

R	**Listen and look. There is one example.**
Mch	I went to a birthday party last week. I took this photo!
F	Yes, it's lovely. Did you have a good time?
Mch	Yes. Can you see the boy with the blonde hair who's eating birthday cake?
F	The boy with a monster on his t-shirt?
Mch	Yes, well, he's my cousin. He's called David. It was his birthday.
R	**Can you see the line? This is an example. Now you listen and draw lines.**
F	It looks like a fun party! Who are the two babies under the table? Do you know their names?
Mch	I don't know the one on the left, but the one on the right who's holding a doll is called Lucy. She was very funny!
F	And who are those two boys playing with the balloons?

Part 1
– 5 questions –

Listen and draw lines. There is one example.

Michael   Sue   Harry   Lucy

David   Richard   Anna

76   Test 4, Listening Part 1

Mch	Oh, the shorter one is my brother, Harry.
F	And the taller one?
Mch	That's his new friend from the football club. I can't remember his name.
F	And the woman with long brown hair, who's she?
Mch	The woman cutting the cake?
F	Yes.
Mch	That's my aunt. Her name's Sue. She makes the best cakes!
F	Oh, did she make the birthday cake?
Mch	Yes. It looks lovely!
F	Who's the boy who's dropped his cake? He looks very unhappy!
Mch	He's my cousin Richard. He's only three.
F	Was your sister at the party? Is that her who's talking to the women?
Mch	No, she's the girl who's taking a photo.
F	Oh, yes. Is she the girl that's standing next to the armchair?
Mch	Yes, that's right. She's called Anna. She got that camera for her birthday – she's going to be a photographer!
R	**Now listen to Part One again.**

Answer Key ➤ SB page 76

Part 2
– 5 questions –

Listen and write. There is one example.

SAM'S PROBLEM

Name:	Sam _North_	
1 **Address:**	2 _Seton_ Street	
2 **Age:**	_13 / thirteen_	
3 **Problem:**	his _front_ teeth hurt	
4 **Day problem started:**	_Sunday_	
5 **See dentist at:**	_5.45 / five forty-five_ p.m.	

Listening Part 2
In this part, students listen and write words or numbers in gaps.

■ Warm-up
For suggested warm-up activities see Test 1 page 10.

■ Do the test
Materials: SB page 77, Audio T4P2

1 Ask students to turn to SB page 77. Look at the form together and get students to think about what kind of information is missing.

2 Play the recording and pause it after the example. Go through the example with the class.

3 Play the rest of the recording. The students listen and fill in the missing words on the form.

4 Let the students listen to the audio again. Check answers.

Audioscript
R **Listen and look. There is One example.**

F Good morning. Rushmore Dentist's Surgery. How can I help you?

M Oh, hello. My son needs to see a dentist please.

F OK. Has your son been here before?

M Yes, he has.

F Right. Can I take his name then please?

M Yes, it's Sam North.

F ... North. OK. Thank you.

R **Can you see the answer? Now you listen and write.**

F And what's the address please?

M It's number two, Seton Street.

F Could you spell that for me please?

M Yes, of course. It's S-E-T-O-N.

F Thank you.
Now, how old is your son?

M He's 12. Oh, no actually he's just had his birthday.

F So he's 13 years old then?

M Yes, that's right. Sorry.

F OK. And what's the problem with your son?

M His front teeth hurt. He was playing baseball with some friends and the ball hit him in the mouth. It hurts a lot and he doesn't want to eat anything.

F Oh dear. And when did this happen? Did the problem start today?

M No, it happened at the weekend, on Saturday, no sorry, Sunday. Yes, his teeth started to hurt that evening when he came home.

F All right. Well, the dentist can see your son this afternoon at 4 pm.

M I'll still be at work then. Do you have anything later than that?

F Let me see. Yes, the dentist can see him at 5:45 pm if that's better? I'm afraid we don't have anything else.

M That's fine. Thanks very much.

R **Now listen to Part Two again.**

Answer Key ➤ SB page 77

Listening Part 3

In this part, students listen and match pictures to words or names by writing a letter in the box.

■ Warm-up

For suggested warm-up activities, see Test 1 page 12.

■ Do the test

Materials: SB pages 78 & 79, Audio T4P3

1 Ask students to turn to SB pages 78 & 79. Look at the list of illustrated names and the set of pictures with the class.

2 Play the recording and pause it after the example. Go through the example with the class, making sure they understand what they need to do.

3 Play the rest of the recording. The students listen and match the illustrated names with the pictures, A to H.

4 Let the students listen to the audio again. Check answers.

Audioscript

R   **Listen and look. There is one example.**
   What does each of these people like about their job?

M   What did you do at school today, Sarah?

Fch   We talked to different people about their jobs. They told us what they liked and didn't like doing. The first one was Betty. She's a journalist. She started working at a newspaper but now she writes stories in a popular magazine. She likes that better. Her job sounds very interesting.

R   **Can you see the letter 'F'? Now you listen and write a letter in each box.**

M   Who else did you meet?

Part 3
– 5 questions –

What does each of these people like about their job?
Listen and write a letter in each box. There is one example.

Betty — F
William — A
Robert — G
John — B
Sally — E
Emma — D

78   Test 4, Listening Part 3

Fch   Well, next was John. He's a mechanic. He loves driving and he loves working with cars and motorbikes. He also reads magazines about them! He has to start work early in the morning but he doesn't like that!

M   Who was the third person?

Fch   It was your friend Sally, you know ... the artist. She said she loved painting when she was little and won lots of competitions. She paints pictures of everything .... the countryside, people, flowers ... but she likes painting animals best.

M   Did anyone have an unusual job?

Fch   Yes, next we talked to an astronaut. His name was William. He was very funny. He doesn't like travelling by plane because he feels afraid! What he does like about his job is seeing the stars and planets in the sky.

M   That is an interesting job.

Fch   After that, we met Robert. He's a footballer and he plays for the town team.

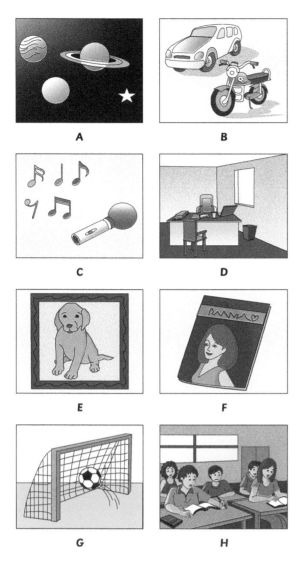

He didn't go to university or have to study but he runs every day and plays matches twice a week. He likes scoring goals best.

M Really? That sounds fun too. Was that everyone?

Fch No, we also met a businesswoman called Emma. She was very friendly. She doesn't like working outside. She prefers working inside, in an office. I think that's a good job too!

R **Now listen to Part Three again.**

Answer Key ➤ SB page 78

Listening Part 4

In this part, students listen and tick the correct picture.

■ Warm-up

For suggested warm-up activities, see Test 1 page 14.

■ Do the test

Materials: SB pages 80 & 81, Audio T4P4

1 Ask students to turn to SB pages 80 & 81. Look at the five questions together and get students to think about what differences they can see in each set of pictures.

2 Play the recording and pause it after the example. Go through the example with the class, making sure they understand what they need to do.

3 Play the rest of the recording. As the students listen to the questions, they look at each set of pictures and tick the correct box, A, B or C.

4 Let students listen to the audio again. Check answers.

Audioscript

R	**Listen and look. There is one example. Which castle did Daisy go to?**
M	Hi, Daisy. What did you do yesterday?
Fch	I went to the castle, grandpa.
M	The castle opposite the park?
Fch	That closed a long time ago! It's opposite the train station.
M	Oh yes, I remember now. It's next to the zoo.
R	**Can you see the tick? Now you listen and tick the box.** **One. Who is Daisy's best friend?**
Fch	I went with my best friend!

M	Who's that?
Fch	Ann. She's got blonde curly hair. I think last time you saw her she had long hair but now it's short.
M	Oh, yes, Ann.
R	**Two. What was Daisy's favourite animal at the zoo?**
Fch	Then, we visited the zoo in the afternoon.
M	Did you have a good time?
Fch	Yes, we had a great time. We saw some funny camels!
M	Were they your favourite?

Fch	Usually the giraffes are my favourite, but this time I thought the kangaroos were the best because they had little babies.
M	Great!
R	**Three. Which hat did Daisy buy?**
Fch	It was very sunny yesterday – and I forgot my hat!
M	Oh dear!
Fch	I bought this new hat with pink flowers on it and my friend bought a pink spotted one.
M	Lovely! I think it's nicer than your old yellow one.

Part 4
– 5 questions –

Listen and tick (✓) the box. There is one example.

Which castle did Daisy go to?

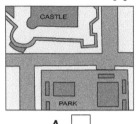 A ☐ 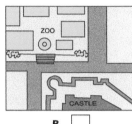 B ☐ 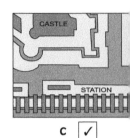 C ✓

1 Who is Daisy's best friend?

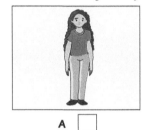 A ☐ 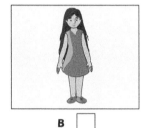 B ☐  C ✓

2 What was Daisy's favourite animal at the zoo?

 A ✓ 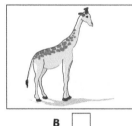 B ☐ 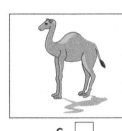 C ☐

80　Test 4, Listening Part 4

3   Which hat did Daisy buy?

A ☐   B ☑   C ☐

4   What did Daisy find at the zoo shop?

 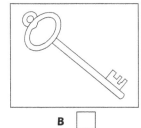 

A ☐   B ☐   C ☑

5   What time did Daisy leave the zoo?

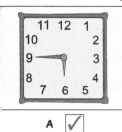 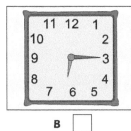 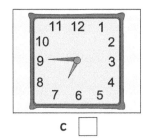

A ☑   B ☐   C ☐

R	**Four. What did Daisy find at the zoo shop?**
Fch	I found something on the floor at the zoo shop.
M	Was it someone's keys?
Fch	No it was a watch! It looked expensive!
M	What did you do?
Fch	I took it to the ticket office.
R	**Five. What time did Daisy leave the zoo?**
M	Did you stay at the zoo all day?
Fch	Yes! It closes at 6:15 and we left at 5:45. I think we were the last people to leave!

M	So were you home for dinner?
Fch	Yes, we were home at 6:45.
R	**Now listen to Part Four again.**

Answer Key ➤ SB pages 80 & 81

Listening Part 5

In this part, students listen and colour, draw and write on a picture.

■ Warm-up

For suggested warm-up activities, see Test 1 page 16.

■ Do the test

Materials: SB page 82, Audio T4P5, coloured pencils

1 Ask students to turn to SB page 82. Look at the picture with the class and ask them to name items and actions in the picture. Explain that they will listen to instructions in the form of a conversation between an adult and a child.

2 Play the recording and pause it after the example. Go through the example with the class. Make sure students understand that they will need to colour three things in the picture, write one word and draw one simple object (and also colour it).

3 Play the rest of the recording. The pupils listen and follow the instructions.

4 Let the students listen to the audio again. Check answers.

Audioscript

R	**Listen and look at the picture.** **There is one example.**
Mch	I like that picture. It's funny!
F	Can you colour it for me then?
Mch	Yes, please. What shall I colour first?
F	Can you see the woman who's washing the plates?
Mch	Yes, she's got long curly hair.
F	That's right. Can you colour her t-shirt red?
Mch	OK.

Part 5
– 5 questions –

Listen and colour and draw and write. There is one example.

82 Test 4, Listening Part 5

R	**Can you see the woman's red t-shirt? This is an example. Now you listen and colour and draw and write.** **One**
F	Good. Now then, there are two women who're holding boxes of vegetables.
Mch	Yes, the woman on the right's taller and she's got carrots in her box.
F	That's right. Do you want to colour the shorter woman's tights?
Mch	OK, what colour?

F	Oh, I don't know, yellow?
Mch	That's an unusual colour!
R	**Two**
F	Now, can you see the waiter who's walking out of the door?
Mch	Yes, he's wearing glasses.
F	That's right, and he's carrying a bowl of soup.
Mch	Yes. Do you want me to colour it?
F	No, I'd like you to draw another bowl of soup next to it.
Mch	OK. I've done it! I'll colour it orange.

R	**Three**
F	Can you see the small bag?
Mch	Yes, it's on top of the fridge where the woman is washing the plates.
F	That's right. Well, can you write the word SALT on it?
Mch	I'm doing that now.
F	Right.

R	**Four**
F	Good. Can you see the two cooks?
Mch	Yes, they're both wearing funny hats!
F	Well, one of the cooks is looking at the waiter who has dropped some glasses.
Mch	Oh yes, he looks very angry!
F	Can you colour his hat blue.
Mch	Yes, OK.

R	**Five**
F	Right. Can you see the spoons that are on the wall?
Mch	Oh yes, there are three. Shall I colour them?
F	Not all of them, just the one on the right next to the clock.
Mch	OK. What colour?
F	You can choose.
Mch	OK. I'll colour it purple.
F	That's a good idea. It looks good!

R	**Now listen to Part Five again.**

Answer Key ➤ SB page 82

Reading & Writing
Part 1

In this part, students write the correct words next to the definitions.

■ Warm-up

For suggested warm-up activities, see Test 1 page 19.

■ Do the test

Materials: SB page 83

1 Ask students to turn to SB page 83. Look at the fifteen individual words and get students to think about what they mean.

2 Ask students to read through the ten definitions. Look at the example together.

3 Ask the students to match the definitions with the correct words. Remind them to copy the words carefully.

4 Check the answers.

Answer Key ➤ SB page 83

Part 1
– 10 questions –

Look and read. Choose the correct words and write them on the lines. There is one example.

an actress   caves   an engineer   deserts

a uniform

a scarf

queens

a pyramid

shorts   a secretary   a nose

a belt

a hill

an umbrella

a leg

You wear this around your neck when it is cold. — **a scarf**

1 These are very rich women who sometimes live in castles. — **queens**

2 You wear this so that your trousers don't fall down. — **a belt**

3 This person works in an office and often answers the phone. — **a secretary**

4 These are large, hot places where it doesn't rain a lot. — **deserts**

5 You can find these in mountains. Animals like bears live in them. — **caves**

6 This is something you can climb which isn't as high as a mountain. — **a hill**

7 These are clothes that people often wear for their job. — **a uniform**

8 We use this part of our body to smell things. — **a nose**

9 Girls or boys can wear these. They are good in the summer when it's hot. — **shorts**

10 You can see this woman in the cinema or the theatre. — **an actress**

Test 4, Reading & Writing Part 1   83

Part 2

– 7 questions –

Look and read. Write **yes** or **no**.

Examples

The woman is making a cake with butter, sugar and flour.

_____yes_____

The little girl with the curly hair is wearing blue shorts.

_____no_____

Reading & Writing
Part 2

In this part, students look at a picture and then read sentences and write yes or no answers.

■ Warm-up

For suggested warm-up activities, see Test 1 page 20.

■ Do the test

Materials: SB pages 84 & 85

1 Ask students to turn to SB pages 84 & 85. Look at the picture together.

2 Ask students to look at the two examples and discuss these with the class. Ask them to correct the second example, e.g. _The little girl with curly hair is wearing red shorts._

3 The students now decide whether the information in the other seven sentences about the picture are correct. Remind pupils to write either _yes_ or _no_ after each sentence. Ask students to correct the false sentences. (1 _The man who is cooking has got a green belt._ 3 _The old woman isn't giving the baby some milk._ 5 _There are some knives and forks next to a bottle._)

Answer Key ➤ SB page 85

Questions

1   The man who is cooking eggs has got a grey belt.   _no_

2   There is a radio on the shelf which is next
    to the mirror.   _yes_

3   The old woman is giving the baby some milk.   _no_

4   The little boy who is next to the computer
    looks unhappy.   _yes_

5   There are some knives and forks in front of
    a bottle.   _no_

6   Someone has put some bowls and glasses on
    the table.   _yes_

7   More than one of the children has got brown hair.   _yes_

Part 3
– 5 questions –

Jane is talking to her friend, Alex. What does Alex say?

Read the conversation and choose the best answer.
Write a letter (A–H) for each answer.

You do not need to use all the letters.

Example

	Jane:	Hi, Alex. Have you met the new girl in your class yet?
	Alex:	_____ D _____

Questions

1   Jane: Do you know where she comes from?

    Alex: _____ H _____

2   Jane: Has she got any brothers or sisters?

    Alex: _____ B _____

3   Jane: Does she know anyone at the school?

    Alex: _____ C _____

4   Jane: We should ask her to sit with us at lunchtime.

    Alex: _____ G _____

5   Jane: OK. Shall I meet you both at lunchtime then?

    Alex: _____ E _____

Reading & Writing
Part 3

In this part, students read a dialogue and select the correct response.

■ Warm-up

For suggested warm-up activities, see Test 1 page 20.

■ Do the test

Materials: SB pages 86 & 87

1 Ask students to turn to SB pages 86 & 87. Look at the gapped dialogue together and get students to think about what could go in the gaps.

2 Ask students to read the missing lines of the dialogue, options A–H.

3 Ask students to choose the appropriate line of dialogue from the options given and to write the correct letter in the space provided. Remind them that there is one extra line of dialogue that is not needed. Encourage students to read through the dialogue, quietly to themselves, to check that it makes sense.

4 Check answers.

Answer Key ➤ SB page 86

Test 4

A	There's a new girl in my class.
B	No, she hasn't.
C	No, I don't think she has any friends here.
D	Yes, her name's Daisy. **(Example)**
E	OK – great! See you later.
F	No, she didn't.
G	That's a good idea.
H	She's from a village in the mountains.

Part 4
– 6 questions –

Read the story. Choose a word from the box. Write the correct word next to numbers 1–5. There is one example.

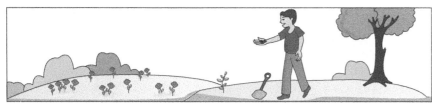

My name's Harry. Last week something very _____*interesting*_____ happened to me.

I went to visit my grandma after school. It was my grandma's birthday and we

gave her a pear tree for her garden. I **(1)** _____*took*_____ the tree into the

garden and put it in the ground. It was hard work and I got very dirty.

Suddenly I saw something in the ground. It was some **(2)** _____*money*_____ .

I took it inside and showed it to my mum and grandma. They said, "It looks

very old! You should take it to the **(3)** _____*museum*_____ ."

The next day I **(4)** _____*went*_____ to town with the old money. The man at

the museum looked very surprised when he saw the money and said, "This is very,

very old. Can we keep it in the museum?" "Of course," I said. The man thanked

me and **(5)** _____*gave*_____ me free family tickets to the museum.

I can't wait to go back to grandma's garden to look for more old treasure!

Reading & Writing
Part 4

In this part, students choose and copy missing words from a story and then choose the best title.

■ Warm-up

For suggested warm-up activities, see Test 1 page 24.

■ Do the test

Materials: SB pages 88 & 89

1. Ask students to turn to SB pages 88 & 89. Look at the picture together and get students to think about the topic of the story.

2. Look at the example with the class and make sure they understand that they need to fill the gaps in the text from the words in the box. Remind students that there are more words than they need.

3. Ask students to fill in the five gaps in the story and to choose the best title for the story from the three options.

4. Check answers.

Answer Key ➤ SB pages 88 & 89

Example				
interesting	made	museum	visit	gave
went	tree	money	airport	took

(6) Now choose the best name for the story.

Tick one box

Grandma's birthday ☐

Treasure in the garden ☑

The trip to town ☐

Part 5

– 7 questions –

Look at the picture and read the story. Write some words to complete the sentences about the story. You can use 1, 2, 3 or 4 words.

Dinosaur fun!

My name's Katy and I love sweets! My favourite ones are called 'Dinosaur Sweets'. Each sweet looks like a dinosaur and they taste of different kinds of fruit. Last month I visited my grandpa and he bought me a big bag of dinosaur sweets. On the back of the bag it said there was a competition. For the competition, you had to paint a picture of a dinosaur. I love painting and so I got my paints out and did a picture. My dinosaur was blue and purple and had big orange teeth! I sent my picture to the address on the bag of sweets the next day.

I forgot about the competition and then three weeks later a woman phoned me. She said, "I have some good news for you. You have won the painting competition!" I couldn't believe it! I was very surprised.

I won lots of great things. They sent me a Dinosaur backpack, T-shirt and pencil case for my prize. They also invited me and my family to visit the factory where they make the sweets. It was very exciting and they gave me and my sister lots of sweets! The best thing is that my picture is now on the front of every bag of Dinosaur Sweets!

Reading & Writing
Part 5

In this part, students complete sentences about a story using one, two or three words.

■ Warm-up

For suggested warm-up activities, see Test 1 page 26.

■ Do the test

Materials: SB pages 90 & 91

1 Ask students to turn to SB pages 90 & 91. Look at the picture and get students to think about the topic of the story.

2 Ask students to read the story and then read the sentences. Then ask the students to underline the parts of the story that give them the information they need to complete the sentences.

3 Look at the example with the class and make sure they understand that they need to fill the gapped sentences using between one and four words. Remind the students that the words they will need to use will be in the story but may not be in the same order as the sentence.

4 Ask students to complete the gapped sentences.

5 Check the answers.

Answer Key ➤ SB page 91

Test 4

Examples

Dinosaur Sweets are Katy's _____*favourite*_____ sweets.

Every sweet tastes of a different kind of fruit and looks _____*like a dinosaur*_____ .

Questions

1   Katy's _____*grandpa*_____ bought her a big bag of Dinosaur Sweets.

2   Katy _____*did / painted*_____ a picture of a dinosaur for the competition.

3   The dinosaur in the picture had _____*big orange teeth*_____ .

4   There was an _____*address*_____ on the bag of sweets which Katy sent her painting to.

5   A woman phoned Katy _____*three weeks*_____ after she sent her picture.

6   Katy won a pencil case, a T-shirt and _____*a dinosaur backpack*_____ .

7   Katy thought that the visit to the factory was _____*very exciting*_____ .

Part 6
– 10 questions –

Read the text. Choose the right words and write them on the lines.

Life under the sea

Example	We still have a lot to learn _____about_____ life under the
1	sea. Do you know that _____more_____ people go into
	space than visit the bottom of our biggest seas!
2	The biggest animals _____that_____ live in the sea are
3	whales. Blue whales are _____the_____ biggest kind and
	they are much bigger than any dinosaurs that ever lived!
4	A lot of the fish we eat comes _____from_____ the sea.
5	Fishing in the sea is _____both_____ a job and a hobby in
	countries all over the world. When people think of the most
6	dangerous fish in the sea, they _____usually_____ think of
7	sharks. Most people are afraid of sharks _____because_____ of
8	stories in books and films. _____There_____ are more than
	350 different kinds of sharks but only a few are dangerous to man.
9	Dolphins also _____live_____ in the sea and most people
10	love to see them. Dolphins _____are_____ very friendly and
	clever and often enjoy swimming with people.

92   Test 4, Reading & Writing Part 6

Reading & Writing Part 6

In this part, students complete a text by selecting and copying the correct words.

■ Warm-up

For suggested warm-up activities, see Test 1 page 28.

■ Do the test

Materials: SB pages 92 & 93

1 Ask students to turn to SB pages 92 & 93. Look at the picture and get students to think about the topic of the text.

2 Go through the example.

3 Ask students to read the text and then read the word options.

4 Ask students to complete the gaps with a word.

5 Check the answers.

Answer Key ➤ SB page 92

Example	about	for	with
1	much	more	many
2	where	what	that
3	the	a	an
4	under	to	from
5	both	all	any
6	never	usually	once
7	than	because	so
8	There	These	They
9	lives	living	live
10	have	see	are

Part 7

– 5 questions –

Read the diary and write the missing words. Write one word on each line.

Monday 4ᵗʰ September

Example I met my new Geography teacher today. She's ___called___

Miss Reece and she's very different to our old teacher!

1 She doesn't like anyone speaking in the _class / classroom_ .

2 We all have to stand up _when / if_ she comes

in the room. The boys in my class don't like her because they

3 can't ___be___ naughty any more!

4 The lesson today was about storms. It ___was___

5 very interesting. ___The___ only problem with

Miss Reece is that she gives us too much homework!

Reading & Writing
Part 7

In this part, students complete a text with words of their own choice.

■ Warm-up

For suggested warm-up activities, see Test 1 page 30.

■ Do the test

Materials: SB page 94

1 Ask students to turn to SB page 94. Look at the gapped text together and get students to think about what sort of words are missing.

2 Look at the example together and ask students to identify whether it is a noun, verb, adjective, etc.

3 Ask students to complete each gap in the text with the missing word.

4 Check answers.

Answer Key ➤ SB page 94

Speaking Part 1

In this part, students identify and describe differences between two pictures.

■ Warm-up

For suggested warm-up activities, see Test 1 page 31.

■ Do the test

Materials: SB page 96, TB page 138

1 Ask the students some general introductory questions, e.g. *What's your surname? How old are you?*

2 Ask the students to turn to SB page 96. Give them time to look at the picture.

3 Turn to the Examiner's copy (TB page 138). Allow students to look at it briefly.

4 Make statements about your copy of the picture. Encourage the student to say how their picture is different. For example, *In my picture, it's 11:25. (In my picture, it's 10:25.)*

Answer Key

1 there are two birds near the clock / there's one bird

2 the man is wearing a blue uniform / he's wearing a grey uniform

3 man buying a drink is wearing a green hat / brown hat

4 the boy who's eating a banana is standing next to a suitcase / the boy who's eating a banana is sitting on the suitcase

5 girl who's waving has curly hair / has straight hair

6 old man has got a white moustache / has got a white beard

Candidate's copy

Part 1

Find the differences

96 Test 4, Speaking Part 1

Candidate's copy

Information exchange

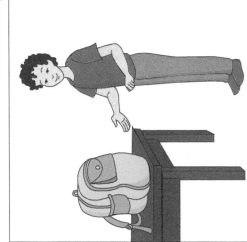

Tony's holiday

Where	?
Who / with	?
How long	?
What / do	?
What / buy	?

Mary's holiday

Where	beach
Who / with	grandparents
How long	2 weeks
What / do	swimming
What / buy	T-shirt

Speaking Part 2

In this part, students ask and answer questions using cues.

■ Warm-up

For suggested warm-up activities, see Test 1 page 32.

■ Do the test

Materials: SB page 97, TB page 139

1 Ask students to turn to SB page 97. Give them time to look at the pictures and the tables.

2 Look at the Examiner's copy (TB page 139). Ask the student questions about the information they have, e.g. *I don't know anything about Mary's holiday. Where did she go? (the beach).*

3 Now encourage the student to ask you similar questions, e.g. *Where did Tony go?*

Answer Key ➤ Speaking frame page 107

Speaking Part 3

In this part, students continue a story by describing the pictures in sequence.

■ Warm-up

For suggested warm-up activities, see Test 1 page 33.

■ Do the test

Materials: SB page 98

1 Ask students to turn to SB page 98. Give them time to look at the pictures first.

2 Tell them the title and then describe the first picture, e.g. *These pictures tell a story. It's called 'The hungry birds'. A family is spending a day on the beach.* etc.

3 Encourage the students to continue the story by describing the other pictures in turn. If necessary prompt them with a question.

Answer Key ➤ Speaking frame page 107

Speaking Part 4

In this part, students answer questions about themselves, their hobbies and their family or friends.

■ Warm-up

For suggested Warm-up activities, see Test 1 page 34.

■ Do the test

Materials: None

1 Ask the students several questions about themselves, their family or friends. They need only give simple answers, i.e. a phrase or a short sentence.

Now let's talk about your friends.

How often do you see your friends?

Part 3

Examiner's and Candidate's copy

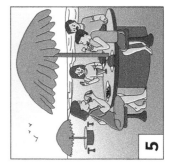

Tell the story

What do you do with your friends after school?

etc.

Speaking frame (Timing = 5–7 minutes)

What to do	What to say	Answer from candidate	Back up question if necessary
	Hello… my name's … *What's your surname?* *How old are you?*	Hello (Fischer) (11)	*What's your family name?* *Are you (11)?*
1 Show candidate both Find the Differences pictures. Point to the birds near the clock in each picture.	*Here are two pictures. My picture is nearly the same as yours, but some things are different.* *For example, in my picture there are two birds near the clock, but in your picture there is only one bird.* *I'm going to say something about my picture. You tell me how your picture is different.* *In my picture the man talking to the old woman is wearing a blue uniform.* *In my picture, the time is twenty-five past eleven.* *In my picture, the man buying a drink is wearing a green hat.* *In my picture, the boy eating a banana is standing next to the suitcase.* *In my picture, the girl who is waving has got curly hair.* *In my picture, the old man has got a white moustache.*	In my picture, the man talking to the old woman is wearing a grey uniform. In my picture, the time is twenty-five past ten. In my picture, the man is wearing an brown hat. In my picture, the boy eating a banana is sitting on the suitcase. In my picture, the girl who is waving has got straight hair. In my picture, the old man has got a white beard.	Point to the other differences which the student does not mention. *Is the man wearing a blue uniform?* *Is the time twenty past eleven?* *Is the man wearing a green hat?* *Is the boy eating a banana standing next to the suitcase?* *Does the girl who is waving have curly hair?* *Has the old man got a white moustache?*
2 Point to both candidate's and examiner's copies. Point to the picture of the girl before asking the questions. Point to the picture of the boy.	*Mary and Tony have both been on holiday. I don't know anything about Mary's holiday, but you do. So I'm going to ask you some questions.* *Where did Mary go on holiday?* *Who did Mary go with?* *How long did she go there for?* *What did she do there?* *What did she buy there?* *Now you don't know anything about Tony's holiday, so you ask me some questions.* *(To the mountains)* *(His parents)* *(One week)* *(He went skiing)* *(A scarf)*	 To the beach Her grandparents 2 weeks She went swimming. A t-shirt Where did Tony go on holiday? Who did he go with? How long did he go there for? What did he do there? What did he buy there?	Point to the information if necessary. Point to the information if necessary.
3 Point to the picture story. Allow time to look at the pictures.	*These pictures tell a story.* *It's called 'The hungry birds'. Just look at the pictures first.* *A family is spending a day on the beach. They are putting their towels and bags on the beach.* *Now you tell the story.*	2 – The family are going for a swim in the sea. Everyone is laughing and looks very happy. 3 – There are three birds on the towels. They are eating the family's sandwiches. 4 – The family have come out of the sea. The birds have flown away. The parents look angry because the birds have eaten the sandwiches. 5 – The family has gone to a beach café to have lunch. They are eating burgers and chips. The children look very happy. I think they are pleased the birds ate their sandwiches.	*What is the family doing?* *How do you think the family feels?* *How many birds are there?* *What are the birds doing?* *Where are the birds?* *How do the parents feel? Why?* *Where is the family now?* *What are they eating?* *How do the children feel?*
4 Put away all pictures. Ask a few personal questions.	*Now let's talk about friends.* *How often do you see your friends?* *What do you do with your friends after school?* *Where do you go with your friends at the weekend?* *What food do you like to eat with your friends?* *Tell me about your best friend.* *OK, thank you (name).* *Goodbye.*	Every day Play football To the park Chips My best friend's Tom. He's 14 years old. We go to school together. Goodbye.	*Do you see your friends every day?* *Do you play sport with your friends after school?* *Do you go to the park with your friends at the weekend?* *Do you like to eat chips with your friends?* *Who's your best friend? How old is he / she? What do you do together?*

Test 5

Listening Part 1

In this part, students listen and draw lines to match names to people in a picture.

■ Warm-up

For suggested warm-up activities, see Test 1 page 8.

■ Do the test

Materials: SB page 100, Audio T5P1

1 Ask students to turn to SB page 100. Look at the picture together and get students to read the names.
2 Play the recording and pause it after the example. Go through the example with the class.
3 Play the rest of the recording. The students draw a line from the names to the appropriate people in the picture.
4 Let the students listen to the audio again. Check answers.

Audioscript

R	**Listen and look. There is one example.**
Fch	I went on holiday last week. Do you want to see this photo of our hotel?
M	Yes, it's great. Did you have a good holiday?
Fch	Yes, it was lots of fun! Can you see the girl looking at the map?
M	The one who's got a green rucksack?
Fch	Yes, well, her name's Vicky. She was on holiday with her brother.
R	**Can you see the line? This is an example. Now you listen and draw lines.**
M	Who's that man there? The one who looks angry.
Fch	The man in the purple jacket?
M	Yes, he's pointing at those boys.
Fch	Oh, he worked at the hotel. He's called Richard. He isn't happy with the boys because they're getting water all over the floor.
M	Yes, I can see that! Who's the boy with the black hair?
Fch	I'm not sure. But the other boy's called Peter. Can you

Part 1
– 5 questions –

Listen and draw lines. There is one example.

Vicky   William   Sarah   Peter

Betty   Richard   Jane

100   Test 5, Listening Part 1

	see the yellow crocodile he's holding? I've got one like that – it's lots of fun to play with in the sea.
M	I'm sure!
Fch	Can you see the woman who's working behind the hotel desk?
M	Which one? The one who's speaking on the phone?
Fch	No, the other younger woman. Her name's Betty. She talked to us every morning. She was very friendly.
M	And who's the man who's getting his keys?
Fch	The man with the two suitcases? He's called William. Those are his two daughters. Their mum isn't in the picture. I think she

	was getting something from the car.
M	Were his daughters nice?
Fch	Yes. The younger one was very quiet, but I talked to the older girl a lot.
M	Is the older girl the one who's holding the ball with blue and white stripes?
Fch	Yes, and she's got longer hair than her sister. Her name's Sarah. She was nice and very funny!
M	It looks like the hotel was a good place to stay.
Fch	Yes, it was! Mum and dad say we can go back next year!
R	**Now listen to Part One again.**

Answer Key ➤ SB page 100

Part 2
– 5 questions –

Listen and write. There is one example.

SCHOOL ZOO TRIP

	Oldest animal:	*Camel*
1	Age:	*55 / fifty-five*
2	Name:	*Gobi*
3	Likes eating:	*grass*
4	Lives next to:	*giraffes*
5	When children can see him:	after *lunch*

Listening Part 2

In this part, students listen and write words or numbers in gaps.

■ Warm-up

For suggested warm-up activities see Test 1 page 10.

■ Do the test

Materials: SB page 101, Audio T5P2

1 Ask students to turn to SB page 101. Look at the form together and get students to think about what kind of information is missing.

2 Play the recording and pause it after the example. Go through the example with the class.

3 Play the rest of the recording. The students listen and fill in the missing words on the form.

4 Let the students listen to the audio again. Check answers.

Audioscript

R **Listen and look. There is one example.**

F Hello everyone. I hope you're all enjoying your trip to our zoo. Now, I'd like to tell you about the oldest animal in the zoo. Does anyone know what animal it is?

Mch I do, I do!

F OK. What do you think?

Mch I think I read it somewhere. Is it a camel?

F Yes, very good!

R **Can you see the answer? Now you listen and write.**

Mch Can I ask you some questions about the camel?

F Yes, of course! What would you like to know?

Mch How old is the camel?

F Well, they usually live for 40 to 50 years, but our camel is 55 years old, so that's very old!

Mch Wow!
What's the camel called?

F He's called Gobi. That's spelt G-O-B-I.

Mch That's a strange name!

F It's the name of the desert where he comes from.

Mch Oh, right.
What does he like eating?

F He likes eating grass and drinking water.

Mch Can we see the camel? Where does he live in the zoo?

F He lives next to the giraffes. It's not far from here. He likes people and is very friendly. He lives with five other camels and one baby camel.

Mch When can we go and see him?

F Well, you're all going to have lunch now, but you can see him after lunch.

Mch Great! I can't wait! I want to take a photo. Is that OK?

F Yes, that's fine. Now, does anyone else have a question? ... Well, enjoy the rest of your visit.

R **Now listen to Part Two again.**

Answer Key ➤ SB page 101

Listening Part 3

In this part, students listen and match pictures to words or names by writing a letter in the box.

■ Warm-up

For suggested warm-up activities, see Test 1 page 12.

■ Do the test

Materials: SB pages 102 & 103, Audio T5P3

1 Ask students to turn to SB pages 102 & 103. Look at the list of illustrated words and the set of pictures with the class.

2 Play the recording and pause it after the example. Go through the example with the class, making sure they understand what they need to do.

3 Play the rest of the recording. The students listen and match the illustrated words with the pictures, A to H.

4 Let the students listen to the audio again. Check answers.

Audioscript

R **Listen and look. There is one example. Where are the things that Katy wants to take to school?**

F Are you ready Katy? It's eight o'clock – you're going to be late for school!

Fch OK, mum. I haven't brushed my hair yet and I can't find my brush anywhere. I want to take my brush to school. Oh, I remember ... it's on the sofa in the living room.

R **Can you see the letter 'D'? Now you listen and write a letter in each box.**

F Are you ready now?

Fch Not yet, mum, I haven't got my Maths book. I think

Part 3
– 5 questions –

Where are the things that Katy wants to take to school?
Listen and write a letter in each box. There is one example.

brush	D
a letter	E
an umbrella	C
maths book	G
shorts	F
a magazine	A

it's on the telephone table. Oh, no, I remember now, I moved it when I phoned grandma. I put it on the top shelf of the bookcase.

F Are you playing hockey after school today?

Fch Oh, yes. I need my shorts. I want the new white ones that we bought last weekend. They're over there on top of the cupboard by the door with the other clean clothes. I'll go and get them.

F OK but do it quickly! Is there anything else you need?

Fch Yes, I need the letter you wrote for my teacher about the guitar lessons. I found it on the floor under my bed yesterday, but then I picked it up and put it in my rucksack. It's in the front pocket. Ah ... yes, here it is!

F What are you doing now?

Fch I'm looking for my magazine. The one about horses. I've just remembered my friend Emma wants to read it. I know, it's still in the car. I was reading it when we came home from grandma's house yesterday.

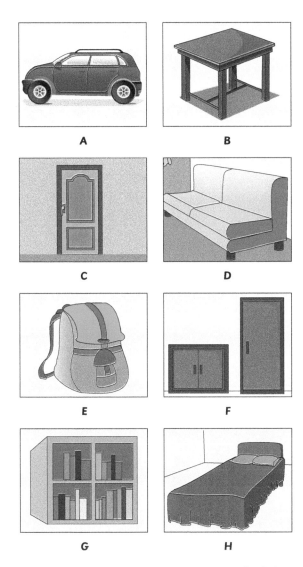

A

B

C

D

E

F

G

H

Test 5, Listening Part 3   103

F   OK, great! Are you ready?

Fch   No, it's going to rain later today. I'm going to take my umbrella but I don't know where it is. I'll go upstairs and look for it. Oh, look there it is – next to the front door.

F   Great! Let's get in the car before you remember anything else!

R   **Now listen to Part Three again.**

Answer Key ➤ SB page 102

Listening Part 4

In this part, students listen and tick the correct picture.

■ Warm-up

For suggested warm-up activities, see Test 1 page 14.

■ Do the test

Materials: SB pages 104 & 105, Audio T5P4

1 Ask students to turn to SB pages 104 & 105. Look at the five questions together and get students to think about what differences they can see in each set of pictures.

2 Play the recording and pause it after the example. Go through the example with the class, making sure they understand what they need to do.

3 Play the rest of the recording. As the students listen to the questions, they look at each set of pictures and tick the correct box, A, B or C.

4 Let students listen to the audio again. Check answers.

Audioscript

R	**Listen and look. There is one example.**
	When is Helen's party going to be?
M	Are you going to have a party for your birthday, Helen?
Fch	Yes, Uncle David. It's going to be on Sunday.
M	Isn't your birthday on Friday?
Fch	Yes, but we're going to stay at grandma's until Saturday.
R	**Can you see the tick? Now you listen and tick the box.**
	One. Where is Helen going to have her party?
M	Are you going to have your party at your house?

Part 4
– 5 questions –

Listen and tick (✓) the box. There is one example.

When is Helen's party going to be?

 A ☐
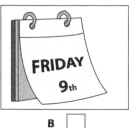 B ☐
 C ✓

1 Where is Helen going to have her party?

 A ✓
 B ☐
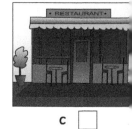 C ☐

2 How many people has Helen invited?

 A ☐
 B ✓
 C ☐

Fch	No, it's too small so we're going to have it at the tennis club.
M	The one opposite that nice restaurant?
Fch	Yes, that's right.
R	**Two. How many people has Helen invited?**
M	Are you going to have a big party?
Fch	Well, last year I invited 30 people, but that was too many.
M	Yes, that is a lot.
Fch	So I've invited 18, but I think only 15 can come.

R	**Three. What food is Helen going to have at her party?**
M	What food are you going to have at the party?
Fch	I don't like cakes, so just sandwiches.
M	Are you going to have pizzas? I thought you loved them.
Fch	I do, but it's easier to just have cold food.
R	**Four. What is Helen going to wear at her party?**
M	Are you going to wear your red and white spotted dress at the party?

What food is Helen going to have at her party?

 A ☐

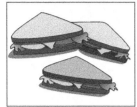 B ☑

 C ☐

What is Helen going to wear at her party?

 A ☐

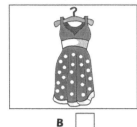 B ☐

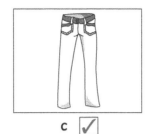 C ☑

What present would Helen like for her birthday?

 A ☐

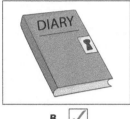 B ☑

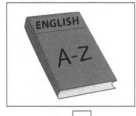 C ☐

Fch I'm too big for that dress now!

M Oh, so have you got a new skirt to wear?

Fch No, I've got some new white jeans.

R **Five. What present would Helen like for her birthday?**

M What would you like for your birthday? I haven't bought your present yet.

Fch I don't know.

M What about some books or a dictionary for school?

Fch I've already got those, but I'd like a new diary.

M That's a good idea. I'll go shopping tomorrow!

R **Now listen to Part Four again.**

Answer Key ➤ SB pages 104 & 105

Listening Part 5

In this part, students listen and colour, draw and write on a picture.

■ Warm-up

For suggested warm-up activities, see Test 1 page 14.

■ Do the test

Materials: SB page 106, Audio T5P5, coloured pencils

1 Ask students to turn to SB page 106. Look at the picture with the class and ask them to name items and actions in the picture. Explain that they will listen to instructions in the form of a conversation between an adult and a child.

2 Play the recording and pause it after the example. Go through the example with the class. Make sure students understand that they will need to colour three things in the picture, write one word and draw one simple object (and also colour it).

3 Play the rest of the recording. The students listen and follow the instructions.

4 Let the students listen to the audio again. Check answers.

Audioscript

R **Listen and look at the picture.**
There is one example.

M This is a picture of a famous singer. Do you want to colour it?

Fch Yes, please! I'd love to.

M OK, well can you see the woman in the middle who's wearing one glove?

Fch Yes.

M That's the singer. Can you colour her glove green?

Fch Yes.

Part 5
– 5 questions –

Listen and colour and write and draw. There is one example.

106 Test 5, Listening Part 5

R **Can you see the singer's green glove? This is an example. Now you listen and colour and write and draw.**
One

M Now can you see the two men who're playing the guitar?

Fch Yes. The man on the left is wearing funny glasses! Shall I colour them?

M No. Can you colour his guitar?

Fch OK. Can I colour it blue?

M Yes, that's a good colour.

Fch There, I've done it!

R **Two**

M Right, now I'd like you to write something.

Fch OK. What shall I write?

M Can you see the photographer?

Fch Yes, he's taking a picture of the singer.

M Well, I'd like you to write 'news' on his bag.

Fch OK. There!

R **Three**

M Now can you see the stars on the singer's jacket?

Fch	Yes, there are two!
M	That's right. Well can you draw another star on her jacket?
Fch	All right. There it is.
M	Now can you colour it pink?
Fch	I'm doing that now.
R	**Four**
Fch	Look at the man who's playing the drums. Can I colour his beard?
M	Not yet. Can you colour one of the drums?
Fch	Which one? There are three.
M	The smallest drum.
Fch	OK. What colour?
M	Orange, please.
R	**Five**
M	Now, can you see the three girls in front of the stage?
Fch	Yes, they look very excited!
M	Yes. Can you see the tallest girl?
Fch	Yes, she's got long hair.
M	I'd like you to colour it purple.
Fch	OK then.
R	**Now listen to Part Five again.**

Answer Key ➤ SB page 106

Reading & Writing
Part 1

In this part, students write the correct words next to the definitions.

■ Warm-up

For suggested warm-up activities, see Test 1 page 19.

■ Do the test

Materials: SB page 107

1 Ask students to turn to SB page 107. Look at the fifteen individual words and get students to think about what they mean.

2 Ask students to read through the ten definitions. Look at the example together.

3 Ask the students to match the definitions with the correct words. Remind them to copy the words carefully.

4 Check the answers.

Answer Key ➤ SB page 107

Part 1
– 10 questions –

**Look and read. Choose the correct words and write them on the lines.
There is one example.**

a fork   a spoon   stamps   a nurse

These people are both your father and your mother.	parents
1 This is someone who works in a hospital and looks after ill people.	a nurse
2 We use these to cut things. They are often made of metal and plastic.	scissors
3 These are small things that you buy and put on an envelope before you post it.	stamps
4 This is a woman who is married.	a wife
5 These people fly planes and travel round the world a lot.	pilots
6 This is made of metal and we often use it with a knife. It isn't round.	a fork
7 This person writes the stories in a newspaper or magazine.	a journalist
8 This is when two or more people talk to each other.	a conversation
9 This is a group of people who play a sport together.	a team
10 This is something that you can't tell anyone about.	a secret

a secret   an envelope

parents   pilots

a team   a conversation

a journalist   a wife

scissors   a husband   a policeman

Part 2
– 7 questions –

Look and read. Write yes or no.

Examples

The boy who is riding a blue bicycle is
wearing sunglasses. _____yes_____

There are some purple flowers under
the window. _____no_____

Test 5, Reading & Writing Part 2

Reading & Writing
Part 2

In this part, students look at a
picture and then read sentences
and write *yes* or *no* answers.

■ Warm-up

For suggested warm-up
activities, see Test 1 page 20.

■ Do the test

Materials: SB pages 108 & 109

1 Ask students to turn to SB
   pages 108 & 109. Look at the
   picture together.
2 Ask students to look at the
   two examples and discuss
   these with the class. Ask them
   to correct the second example,
   e.g. *There are some yellow flowers
   in the window.*
3 The students now decide
   whether the information in
   the other seven sentences
   about the picture are correct.
   Remind students to write
   either *yes* or *no* after each
   sentence. Ask students to
   correct the false sentences.
   (2 *The woman at the front door
   is wearing a skirt and a shirt.*
   5 *There is one cat.* 6 *One of the
   car doors is open.* 7 *The tree
   which is nearer to the house has
   no apples on it.*)

Answer Key ➤ SB page 109

1   The man who is holding a newspaper is also sleeping.   *yes*

2   The woman at the front door is wearing a dress and grey tights.   *no*

3   The man who is washing the car has got a moustache.   *yes*

4   The girl at the upstairs window is waving.   *yes*

5   There are two cats and one of them is on the car.   *no*

6   All the car doors are closed.   *no*

7   The tree which is nearer to the house has a lot of apples on it.   *no*

Part 3
– 5 questions –

Sally is talking to her friend, David. What does David say?

Read the conversation and choose the best answer.
Write a letter (A–H) for each answer.

You do not need to use all the letters.

Example

| | Sally: | Hi, David. Have you done your English homework yet? |
| | David: | _____ G _____ |

Questions

1   Sally: Remember ... we must read the first fifty pages of our book.

  David: _____ B _____

2   Sally: The book is called "The Dark Sea". Have you got it?

  David: _____ H _____

3   Sally: Do you know what it's about?

  David: _____ A _____

4   Sally: Do you like books about pirates?

  David: _____ D _____

5   Sally: We've got to talk about it in tomorrow's English lesson.

  David: _____ E _____

Reading & Writing
Part 3

In this part, students read a dialogue and select the correct response.

■ Warm-up

For suggested warm-up activities, see Test 1 page 20.

■ Do the test

Materials: SB pages 110 & 111

1 Ask pupils to turn to SB pages 110 & 111. Look at the gapped dialogue together and get students to think about what could go in the gaps.

2 Ask students to read the missing lines of the dialogue, options A–H.

3 Ask students to choose the appropriate line of dialogue from the options given and to write the correct letter in the space provided. Remind them that there is one extra line of dialogue that is not needed. Encourage students to read through the dialogue, quietly to themselves, to check that it makes sense.

4 Check answers.

Answer Key ➤ SB page 110

A   It's about pirates, I think.

B   Oh, yes. I remember now.

C   The homework's too difficult.

D   Yes, they are usually very exciting.

E   OK. I'm going to read it tonight.

F   What are you going to
    read tomorrow?

G   Oh, no! I forgot.   **(Example)**

H   Yes. My mum bought it last week.

Part 4
– 6 questions –

Read the story. Choose a word from the box. Write the correct word next to numbers 1–5. There is one example.

It was time for my science _____lesson_____ at school. I went into the

classroom with my friends and sat down. Our science teacher was a funny man

called Mr Brown. He looked very **(1)** _____excited_____ that morning. He said,

"I want everyone to come outside. I have something very interesting to show you!"

We all went outside and were very surprised to see a big space **(2)** _____rocket_____

in the playground. Mr Brown said, "Today we are going to learn about space".

We all **(3)** _____followed_____ Mr Brown into the rocket. Mr Brown told us to

sit down and hold on. "We're going to travel into space!" he told us with a

big **(4)** _____smile_____ .

Suddenly there was a loud noise and we felt the rocket fly into the sky. Out of

the small window we could see the school below us. A few minutes later we

could see **(5)** _____planets_____ and stars. I started to feel afraid.

Then I heard my mum calling me, "Wake up, Emma! You're going to be late

for school!"

Reading & Writing Part 4

In this part, students choose and copy missing words from a story and then choose the best title.

■ Warm-up

For suggested warm-up activities, see Test 1 page 24.

■ Do the test

Materials: SB pages 112 & 113

1 Ask students to open their SB at pages 112 & 113. Look at the picture together and get students to think about the topic of the story.

2 Look at the example with the class and make sure they understand that they need to fill the gaps in the text from the words in the box. Remind students that there are more words than they need.

3 Ask students to fill in the five gaps in the story and to choose the best title for the story from the three options.

4 Check answers.

Answer Key ➤ SB pages 112 & 113

Example				
lesson	planets	excited	rocket	flew
smile	silver	moon	followed	wonderful

(6) Now choose the best name for the story.

Tick one box

A strange dream ✓

Science is boring! ☐

The astronaut ☐

Part 5

– 7 questions –

Look at the picture and read the story. Write some words to complete the sentences about the story. You can use 1, 2, 3 or 4 words.

My hospital surprise!

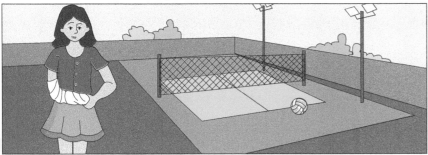

My name is Helen Jones and my favourite sport is volleyball. I play volleyball for the school team and last week we had an important game. In the second half of the game, I fell over and hurt my arm. I couldn't move my arm and it hurt a lot. My sports teacher called for an ambulance and they took me to hospital. The doctors looked at my arm and said, "It's broken". I couldn't believe it! I was sad because I couldn't play volleyball, but also because our school skiing holiday was the next day!

The doctors said, "Sorry, you can't go skiing because you need to stay in hospital for one night". I was so unhappy that night when I thought about the holiday. Then something happened the next day that helped me forget about the holiday.

I was having lunch in the hospital when Robert Black, my favourite volleyball player, walked into the room! He was in hospital to see a doctor about his leg so he decided to visit the children in the hospital. I talked to him about volleyball and a nurse took a photo of us together. That photo's on my bedroom shelf now! It was much more exciting than a skiing holiday!

Reading & Writing Part 5

In this part, students complete sentences about a story using one, two or three words.

■ Warm-up

For suggested warm-up activities, see Test 1 page 26.

■ Do the test

Materials: SB pages 114 & 115

1 Ask students to turn to SB pages 114 & 115. Look at the picture and get students to think about the topic of the story.

2 Ask students to read the story and then read the sentences. Then ask the students to underline the parts of the story that give them the information they need to complete the sentences.

3 Look at the example with the class and make sure they understand that they need to fill the gapped sentences using between one and four words. Remind the students that the words they will need to use will be in the story but may not be in the same order as the sentence.

4 Ask students to complete the gapped sentences.

5 Check the answers.

Answer Key ➤ SB page 115

Test 5

Examples

Helen Jones loves playing ___volleyball___ .

Helen's important volleyball game was ___last week___ .

Questions

1 Helen hurt her arm when she ___fell over___ .

2 An ___ambulance___ took Helen to hospital.

3 Helen had to stay in hospital because her arm ___was broken___ .

4 Helen felt sad because she wanted to go on the ___skiing___ holiday.

5 Helen was ___having lunch___ , when Robert Black walked into the room.

6 Robert Black was in hospital because of a problem with
his ___leg___ .

7 Helen has a photo of her and Robert Black on the ___shelf___
in her bedroom.

Part 6
– 10 questions –

Read the text. Choose the right words and write them on the lines.

Actors

Example	The job of an actor is a job _____*that*_____ many people
1	dream about. Every day we _____*hear*_____ on the radio
2	and TV about the exciting times _____*of*_____ famous
	actors. We read about their big houses, fast cars and expensive
3	clothes. Magazines are full of photos of actors _____*at*_____
	parties and restaurants. It looks fun and easy, but for many
4	actors it's a _____*hard*_____ job.
5	Lots of actors _____*start*_____ acting when they are children.
6	Many actors get _____*their*_____ first job in the theatre.
7	If _____*an*_____ actor is good, he or she might get a job
8	on a TV programme or in a film. Only a _____*few*_____
	actors get rich and famous. Many actors do not have a lot of
9	money and often _____*need*_____ to have a second job.
10	For these people being a famous actor is _____*more*_____
	important than money.

Reading & Writing Part 6

In this part, students complete a text by selecting and copying the correct words.

■ Warm-up
For suggested warm-up activities, see Test 1 page 28.

■ Do the test
Materials: SB pages 116 & 117

1 Ask students to turn to SB pages 116 & 117. Look at the picture and get students to think about the topic of the text.
2 Go through the example.
3 Ask students to read the text and then read the word options.
4 Ask students to complete the gaps with a word.
5 Check the answers.

Answer Key ➤ SB page 116

Example	what	that	where
1	heard	hearing	hear
2	for	of	from
3	on	with	at
4	hard	harder	hardest
5	starting	start	started
6	their	them	they
7	the	a	an
8	small	few	little
9	must	should	need
10	more	much	many

Part 7

– 5 questions –

Read the letter and write the missing words. Write one word on each line.

	Dear Holly,
Example	How are _____*you*_____ ? I went to the cinema
	yesterday. I saw the film "Naughty Nick". I thought the
1	film _____*was*_____ great! I couldn't stop laughing when
2	Nick pushed the girl _____*into*_____ the swimming pool
3	at the party. That was so funny! _____*Have*_____ you
	seen the film yet?
	It's only two weeks until I see you. I can't wait! What kind
4	of _____*clothes*_____ should I take with me? Is the weather
5	hot _____*where*_____ you live? It's raining here!
	Love,
	Katy x

Reading & Writing
Part 7

In this part, students complete a text with words of their own choice.

■ Warm-up

For suggested warm-up activities, see Test 1 page 30.

■ Do the test

Materials: SB page 118

1 Ask students to turn to SB page 118. Look at the gapped text together and get students to think about what sort of words are missing.

2 Look at the example together and ask students to identify whether it is a noun, verb, adjective, etc.

3 Ask students to complete each gap in the text with the missing word.

4 Check answers.

Answer Key ➤ SB page 118

Speaking Part 1

In this part, students identify and describe differences between two pictures.

■ Warm-up

For suggested warm-up activities, see Test 1 page 31.

■ Do the test

Materials: SB page 120, TB page 140

1 Ask the students some general introductory questions, e.g. *What's your surname? How old are you?*

2 Ask the students to turn to SB page 120. Give them time to look at the picture.

3 Turn to the Examiner's copy (TB page 140). Allow students to look at it briefly.

4 Make statements about your copy of the picture. Encourage the student to say how their picture is different. For example, *In my picture, the man in the hat is selling newspapers.* (*In my picture, he's selling flowers.*)

Answer Key

1 man riding bike is wearing black gloves / grey gloves

2 it's 2:45 / it's 4:30

3 policewoman next to tree / nurse next to tree

4 woman and baby going into chemist / woman and baby coming out of chemist

5 girl holding a blue & yellow balloon / a yellow and purple balloon

6 boys running after a dog / running after a butterfly

Candidate's copy

Part 1

Find the differences

120　Test 5, Speaking Part 1

Candidate's copy

Part 2

Information exchange

Sam's pet

Kind of animal	cat
How old	5
What / called	Timmy
Like / eat	fish
What colour	black

Daisy's pet

Kind of animal	?
How old	?
What / called	?
Like / eat	?
What colour	?

Test 5, Speaking Part 2 121

Speaking Part 2

In this part, students ask and answer questions using cues.

■ Warm-up

For suggested warm-up activities, see Test 1 page 32.

■ Do the test

Materials: SB page 121, TB page 141

1 Ask students to trun to SB page 121. Give them time to look at the pictures and the tables.

2 Look at the Examiner's copy (TB page 141). Ask the student questions about the information they have, e.g. *I don't know anything about Sam's pet. What kind of animal is it?* (a cat.)

3 Now encourage the student to ask you similar questions, e.g. *How old is Daisy's pet?*

Answer Key ➤ Speaking frame page 131

Speaking Part 3

In this part, students continue a story by describing the pictures in sequence.

■ Warm-up

For suggested warm-up activities, see Test 1 page 33.

■ Do the test

Materials: SB page 122

1 Ask students to turn to SB page 122. Give them time to look at the pictures first.

2 Tell them the title and then describe the first picture, e.g. *These pictures tell a story. It's called 'The football game'. A boy is going to play football.* etc.

3 Encourage the students to continue the story by describing the other pictures in turn. If necessary prompt them with a question.

Answer Key ➤ Speaking frame page 131

Speaking Part 4

In this part, students answer questions about themselves, their hobbies and their family or friends.

■ Warm-up

For suggested Warm-up activities, see Test 1 page 34.

■ Do the test

Materials: None

1 Ask the students several questions about themselves, their family or friends. They need only give simple answers, i.e. a phrase or a short sentence.

Now let's talk about shopping. How often do you go shopping? Who do you usually go shopping with?

etc.

Examiner's and Candidate's copy

Part 3

Tell the story

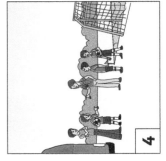

122   Test 5, Speaking Part 3

Speaking frame   (Timing = 5–7 minutes)

What to do	What to say	Answer from candidate	Back up question if necessary
	Hello..., my name's ... *What's your surname?* *How old are you?*	*Hello* *(Fischer)* *(11)*	*What's your family name?* *Are you (11)?*
1 Show candidate both Find the differences pictures. Point to the man on the bike in each picture.	*Here are two pictures. My picture is nearly the same as yours, but some things are different.* *For example, in my picture the man riding a bike is wearing black gloves, but in your picture he's wearing grey gloves.* *I'm going to say something about my picture. You tell me how your picture is different.* *In my picture, the man in the hat is selling newspapers.* *In my picture, the time is two forty five.* *In my picture, there is a policewoman standing next to the tree.* *In my picture, a woman with a baby is going into the chemist.* *In my picture, the girl is holding a blue and a yellow balloon.* *In my picture, the boys are running after a dog.*	*In my picture, the man in the hat is selling flowers.* *In my picture, the time is four thirty.* *In my picture, there is a nurse standing next to the tree.* *In my picture, a woman with a baby is coming out of the chemist.* *In my picture, the girl is holding a purple and a yellow balloon.* *In my picture, the boys are running after a butterfly.*	Point to the other differences which the student does not mention. *Is the man in the hat selling newspapers?* *Is the time two forty five?* *Is there a policewoman standing next to the tree?* *Is the woman with a baby is going into the chemist?* *Is the girl holding a blue and a yellow balloon?* *Are the boys running after a dog?*
2 Point to both candidate's and examiner's copies. Point to the picture of the boy before asking the questions. Point to the picture of the girl.	*Sam and Daisy both have pets. I don't know anything about Sam's pet, but you do. So I'm going to ask you some questions.* *What kind of animal is Sam's pet?* *How old is Sam's cat?* *What's his cat called?* *What does Timmy like to eat?* *What colour is Timmy?* *Now you don't know anything about Daisy's pet, so you ask me some questions.* *(A rabbit)* *(3)* *(Betty)* *(Carrots)* *(Grey)*	*A cat* *5* *Timmy* *Fish* *Black* *What kind of animal is Daisy's pet?* *How old is Daisy's rabbit?* *What's her rabbit called?* *What does Betty like to eat?* *What colour is Betty?*	Point to the information if necessary. Point to the information if necessary.
3 Point to the picture story. Allow time to look at the pictures.	*These pictures tell a story.* *It's called 'The football game'. Just look at the pictures first.* *A boy is going to play football. He is leaving home and waving goodbye to his mum.* *Now you tell the story.*	*2 – There is a problem with the car. The boy looks worried because he thinks he's going to be late.* *3 – The man and the boy are running after a bus. They want to catch the bus to get to the football game.* *4 – The boy and his dad caught the bus and have just arrived. They look happy because the game hasn't started yet.* *6 – The football team has won the game. The boy's dad is taking a photograph of the team. Everyone looks very happy.*	*Is the car working?* *How do you think the boy feels?* *What are the man and boy doing?* *What do they want to do?* *How did the boy and his dad get to the football game?* *Has the football game started yet?* *Has the boy's team won the game?* *What is the boy's dad doing?* *How does everyone in the picture feel?*
4 Put away all pictures. Ask a few personal questions.	*Now let's talk about shopping.* *How often do you go shopping?* *Who do you usually go shopping with?* *What was the last thing you bought?* *How do you usually go to the shops?* *Tell me about your favourite shop.* *OK, thank you (name).* *Goodbye.*	*Every month* *My mum* *A t-shirt* *By car* *My favourite shop's called 'City Look'. It sells lots of clothes. I like it because the clothes are cool.* *Goodbye.*	*Do you go shopping every month?* *Do you usually go shopping with your mum?* *Was the last thing you bought a t-shirt?* *Do you usually go to the shops by car?* *What's your favourite shop called?* *What does it sell?* *Why do you like it?*

Part 1

Examiner's copy

Find the differences

Part 2

Information exchange

Examiner's copy

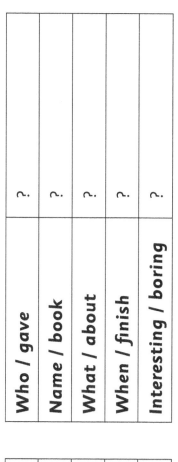

Sarah's book

Who / gave	cousin
Name / book	The Star
What / about	a singer
When / finish	last week
Interesting / boring	interesting

Harry's book

Who / gave	?
Name / book	?
What / about	?
When / finish	?
Interesting / boring	?

Part 1

Find the differences

Part 2

Information exchange

Examiner's copy

Ben's swimming club

What day	Friday
Time	5:15 p.m.
Where	sports centre
How long	1 hour
Teacher	Mrs Crewe

Sarah's tennis club

What day	?
Time	?
Where	?
How long	?
Teacher	?

Part 1

Find the differences

Part 2

Examiner's copy

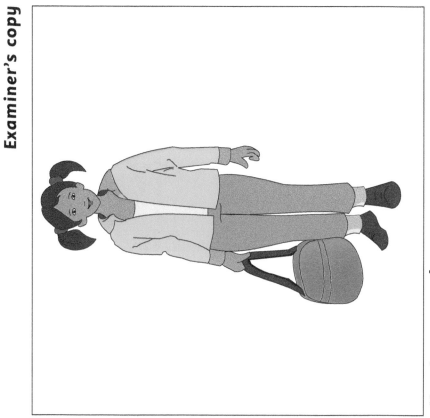

Katy's sports class

Teacher's name	Miss Keen
What day	Friday
What time / start	1:45
How many children	28
What sport / learn	volleyball

Information exchange

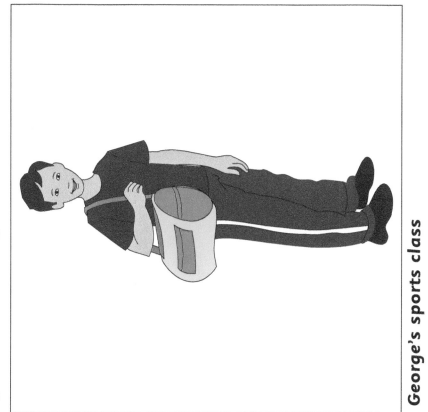

George's sports class

Teacher's name	?
What day	?
What time / start	?
How many children	?
What sport / learn	?

Part 1

Find the differences

Part 2

Information exchange

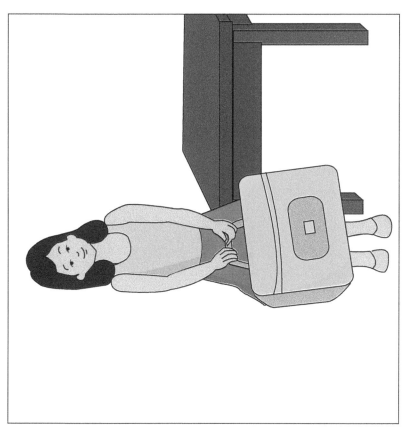

Mary's holiday

Where	?
Who / with	?
How long	?
What / do	?
What / buy	?

Examiner's copy

Tony's holiday

Where	mountains
Who / with	parents
How long	1 week
What / do	skiing
What / buy	scarf

Part 1

Find the differences

Part 2

Information exchange

Examiner's copy

Sam's pet

Kind of animal	?
How old	?
What / called	?
Like / eat	?
What colour	?

Daisy's pet

Kind of animal	rabbit
How old	3
What / called	Betty
Like / eat	carrots
What colour	grey

Worksheet 1

hair	blonde
beard	curly
moustache	straight
thin	fat
belt	shorts
striped	pocket
scarf	sweater
coat	glasses
sitting	lying
smiling	laughing
standing	playing
running	throwing

Worksheet 2

A

TENNIS LESSONS

Time of lesson: **10.45**

Day of lesson: **Tuesday**

Name of teacher: Mrs **White**

Teacher's tel no: **852669**

SWIMMING LESSONS

Time of lesson: _____

Day of lesson: _____

Name of teacher: Mr _____

Teacher's tel no: _____

✂ -

B

TENNIS LESSONS

Time of lesson: _____ .

Day of lesson: _____ .

Name of teacher: Mrs _____

Teacher's tel no: _____

SWIMMING LESSONS

Time of lesson: **9.15**

Day of lesson: **Thursday**

Name of teacher: Mrs **Black**

Teacher's tel no: **377643**

Worksheet 3

Worksheet 4

1

2

3

4

5

Worksheet 5

Worksheet 6

147

Worksheet 7

a dentist	butter	a taxi
an envelope	an umbrella	an ambulance
a waiter	maths	wood
glue	a shelf	fog
an astronaut	an airport	a snack

Worksheet 8

Vicky:	Hi, William. Did you have a good weekend?
William:	Yes thanks, Vicky. I went to the cinema.
Vicky:	Great! What film do you see?
William:	It was called 'Monkeys in space'. Have you seen it?
Vicky:	Not yet, but I want to! Did you go with your mum and dad?
William:	No. My uncle took me.

Jack:	Hi Daisy. What are you doing?
Daisy:	Oh, hi Jack. I'm doing my history homework.
Jack:	I love History. Does Mr Jones teach you history?
Daisy:	No, my teacher's called Mrs Hart. She's really nice. This homework's very difficult.
Jack:	Let me see. Maybe I can help you.
Daisy:	Thanks, Jack.

Ben:	Hi, Emma. Are you going to watch the comedy on TV?
Emma:	I'm not sure Ben. What time does it start?
Ben:	It starts at 2:30 pm.
Emma:	OK. Where are you going to watch it?
Ben:	At my house. Sam's going to come too.
Emma:	Great! I'll see you later.

Worksheet 9

broke	cut	grow	steal	pulled	decided
brushing	leaving	knife	drum	bin	chopsticks
insects	factory	tights	pocket	bored	brave
dry	excellent	friendly	heavy	important	untidy

Read and complete.

1   I _____ a scarf out of my rucksack.

2   He always uses _____ if he is eating rice.

3   I saw that new film yesterday – it was _____ !

4   'Do you like my new spotty _____ ?' asked Vicky.

5   She doesn't like _____ her hair in the morning.

6   He was sorry that he _____ the vase.

7   The new boy at our school is very _____ .

8   There were a lot of _____ in our tent when we went camping!

Worksheet 10

Read and complete.

1   My name is Joe and I have a little brother called Robert.

    Joe has _____ called Robert.

2   Yesterday, Robert and I had chocolate ice cream after lunch.

    Robert and Joe ate some _____ yesterday after lunch.

3   After the ice cream, we took our kite to the park.

    Joe and Robert played with _____ in the park.

4   'You've broken our kite!' I shouted at Robert. I felt very angry.

    Joe was _____ because Robert broke their kite.

5   'It's late. We should go home now,' I said to Robert.

    They went home because it was _____ .

6   Robert said, 'Sorry', and then we went home.

    They went home after Robert _____ .

Worksheet 11

Healthy teeth

If you want healthy teeth you should be careful _____about_____ what you eat and drink. Eat lots of fruit and vegetables and try not to have too _____ sugar. If you _____ a lot of sugar you may get toothache.

You also _____ to brush your teeth twice a day – once after breakfast and once before bedtime. It _____ important to brush all of your teeth, not just _____ front ones. You should spend at least 2 or 3 minutes each time you brush. It is also important to change _____ toothbrush when it gets too old. You should get a new toothbrush _____ 3 months.

Brushing your teeth is important, but you also need to visit your dentist _____ keep your teeth strong and healthy. It's important to visit your dentist twice a year. _____ you visit your dentist he or she will _____ at your teeth to check for any problems.

✂ -

Example	for	<u>about</u>	on
1	many	lots	much
2	eat	ate	eating
3	need	must	should
4	are	be	is
5	the	a	an
6	its	your	their
7	every	all	each
8	for	with	to
9	Since	When	During
10	look	looking	looks

Worksheet 12

Look, read and match.

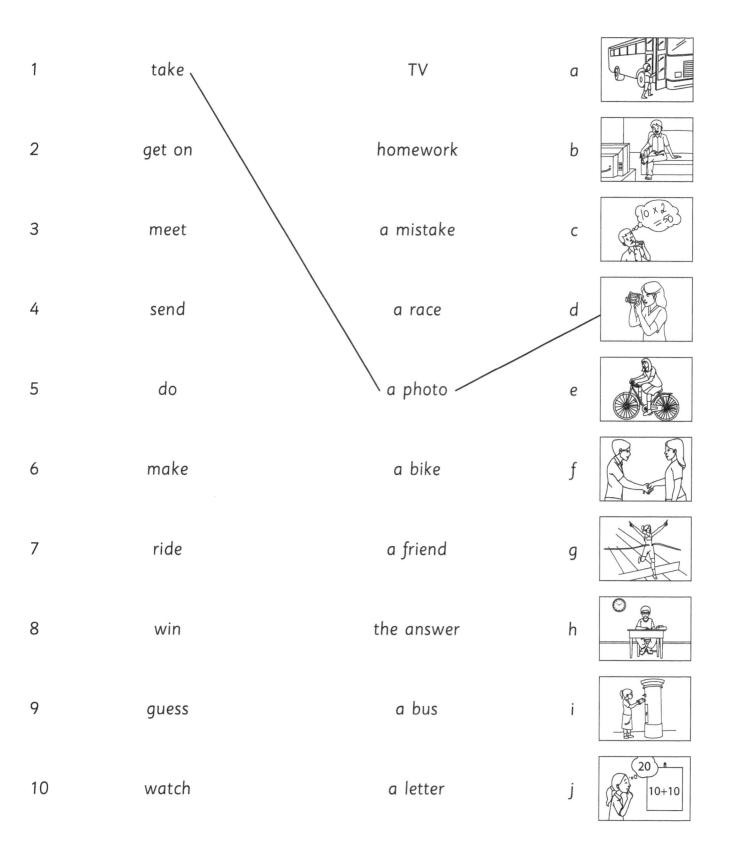

1	take	TV	a	
2	get on	homework	b	
3	meet	a mistake	c	
4	send	a race	d	
5	do	a photo	e	
6	make	a bike	f	
7	ride	a friend	g	
8	win	the answer	h	
9	guess	a bus	i	
10	watch	a letter	j	

Worksheet 13

Monday 9ᵗʰ May

Dear Vicky,

Hi. How _are_ you? It's my birthday soon and I'm (1) _____ a party.

Would (2) _____ like to come? It will be on Saturday 21ˢᵗ May at

7pm (3) _____ Gino's Italian pizza restaurant.

I'm inviting some friends from my school and my cousins. You (4) _____

stay the night at our house on Saturday if you want.

I hope you can come – it will be lots (5) _____ fun.

Love from,
Sally

1 The worst holiday

2 The clever dog

3 The windy day

4 The naughty kitten

5 Snow fun

6 The hockey match

Worksheet 14

Flyers grammar and structures list

Verbs
(Positive, negative, question, imperative and short answer forms including contractions)

Present simple passive (only with 'make' and 'call')

The table is **made of** wood.

Past continuous
I **was walking** down the road when I saw her.

Present perfect
Have you **ever been** to the circus?
He's just **eaten** his dinner.

Be going to
It **isn't going to** rain today.

Will
Will you **do** your homework this evening?
I **won't buy** her a CD because she doesn't like music.

Might
Vicky **might come** to the park.

May
The bus **may** not **come** because there is a lot of snow.

Shall for suggestions
Shall we **have** a picnic in the park?

Could
You **could invite** Robert to the football game.

Should
Should we **take** a towel to the swimming pool?

Tag questions
That's John's book, **isn't it**?

Adverbs
I haven't bought my brother's birthday present **yet**.

Conjunctions
I didn't want to walk home **so** I went on the bus.

If clauses (in zero conditionals)
If it's sunny, **we go swimming**.

Where clauses
My grandmother has forgotten **where she put her glasses**.

Before/after clauses (not with future reference)
I finished my homework **before I played football**.

Be/look/sound/feel/taste/smell like
What's your new teacher **like**?
That sounds like the baby upstairs.

Make somebody/something + adj
That smell **makes me hungry**!

What time ...?
What time does the film start?

What else/next?
What else shall I draw?

See you soon/later/tomorrow, etc.
See you next week, Mrs Ball!

Grammatical Key

adj adjective
adv adverb
conj conjunction
det determiner
dis discourse marker
excl exclamation
int interrogative
n noun
poss possessive
prep preposition
pron pronoun
v verb

A

a.m. (for time)
across *prep*
actor *n*
actually *adv*
adventure *n*
advice *n*
after *adv + conj*
ago *adv*
agree *v*
air *n*
airport *n*
alone *adj*
already *adv*
also *adv*
ambulance *n*
anyone *pron*
anything *pron*
anywhere *adv*
April *n*
arrive *v*
art *n*
artist *n*
astronaut *n*
August *n*
autumn *n* (US fall)
away *adv*

B

backpack *n* (UK rucksack)
before *adv + conj*
begin *v*
believe *v*
belt *n*
Betty *n*
bicycle *n*
bin *n*
biscuit *n* (US cookie)
bit *n*
bored *adj*
brave *adj*
break *v*
bridge *n*
bright *adj* (of colour)
broken *adj*
brush *n + v*
building *n*
burn *v*
business *n*
businessman/woman *n*
butter *n*
butterfly *n*

C

calendar *n*
camel *n*
camp *v*
card *n*
cartoon *n*
castle *n*
cave *n*
centimetre *n* (US centimeter)
century *n*
channel *n*
cheap *adj*
chemist('s) *n*
chess *n*
chopsticks *n*
Christmas *n*
circus *n*

club *n*
collect *v*
college *n*
comb *n + v*
competition *n*
concert *n*
conversation *n*
cook *n*
cooker *n*
cookie *n* (UK biscuit)
corner *n*
could *v* (for possibility)
crown *n*
cut *v*

D

dangerous *adj*
dark *adj*
date *n* (as in time)
David *n*
dear *adj* (as in Dear Harry)
December *n*
decide *v*
dentist *n*
describe *v*
desert *n*
diary *n*
dictionary *n*
dinosaur *n*
drum *n*
during *prep*

E

each *det + pron*
early *adj + adv*
east *n*
else *adv*
Emma *n*
empty *adj*
end *v*
engineer *n*
enough *adj + pron*

entrance *n*
envelope *n*
environment *n*
ever *adv*
everywhere *adv*
exam *n*
excellent *adj + excl*
excited *adj*
exit *n*
expensive *adj*
explain *v*
extinct *adj*

F
fact *n*
factory *n*
fall *n* (UK autumn)
fall over *v*
far *adj + adv*
fast *adj + adv*
February *n*
feel *v*
fetch *v*
a few *det*
find out *v*
finger *n*
finish *v*
fire *n*
fire engine *n* (US fire truck)
fire station *n*
fireman/woman *n*
flag *n*
flashlight *n* (UK torch)
flour *n*
fog *n*
foggy *adj*
follow *v*
footballer *n*
for *prep of time*
forget *v*
fork *n*
fridge *n*
friendly *adj*
front *adj + n*
full *adj*
fun *adj + n*

fur *n*
future *n*

G
gate *n*
geography *n*
George *n*
get married *v*
get to *v*
glass *adj*
glove *n*
glue *n + v*
go out *v*
goal *n*
gold *adj + n*
golf *n*
group *n*
grow *v*
guess *n + v*

H
half *adj + n*
happen *v*
hard *adj + adv*
Harry *n*
hate *v*
headteacher *n*
hear *v*
heavy *adj*
Helen *n*
herself *pron*
high *adj*
hill *n*
himself *pron*
history *n*
Holly *n*
honey *n*
hope *v*
horrible *adj*
hotel *n*
hour *n*
how long *adv + int*
hurry *v*
husband *n*

I
ice *n*
if *conj*
ill *adj*
important *adj*
improve *v*
information *n*
insect *n*
instrument *n*
interesting *adj*
itself *pron*

J
jam *n*
January *n*
job *n*
join *v* (a club)
journalist *n*
journey *n*
July *n*
June *n*
just *adv*

K
Katy *n*
keep *v*
key *n*
kilometre *n* (US kilometer)
kind *adj*
king *n*
knife *n*

L
language *n*
large *adj*
late *adj + adv*
later *adv*
lazy *adj*
leave *v*
left *adj + n* (as in direction)
let *v*
letter *n* (as in mail)
lie *v* (as in lie down)
lift *n* (ride)
lift *v*

light *adj* + *n*
little *adj*
a little *adv* + *det*
London *n*
look after *v*
look like *v*
lovely *adj*
low *adj*
lucky *adj*

M
magazine *n*
make sure *v*
March *n*
married *adj*
match *n* (football)
maths *n* (US math)
May *n*
may *v*
meal *n*
mechanic *n*
medicine *n*
meet *v*
meeting *n*
member *n*
metal *adj* + *n*
metre *n* (US meter)
Michael *n*
midday *n*
middle *n* + *adj*
midnight *n*
might *v*
million *n*
mind *v*
minute *n*
missing *adj*
mix *v*
money *n*
month *n*
much *adv* + *det* + *pron*
museum *n*
myself *pron*

N
necklace *n*
news *n*

newspaper *n*
next *adj* + *adv*
noisy *adj*
no-one *pron*
normal *adj*
north *n*
November *n*
nowhere *adv*

O
o'clock *adv*
October *n*
octopus *n*
of course *adv*
office *n*
once *adv*
online *adj*
other *det* + *pron*
over *adv* + *prep*

P
p.m. (for time)
painter *n*
paper *adj* + *n*
partner *n*
passenger *n*
past *n* + *prep*
path *n*
pepper *n*
perhaps *adv*
photographer *n*
piece *n*
pilot *n*
pizza *n*
planet *n*
plastic *adj* + *n*
player *n*
pocket *n*
police station *n*
policeman/woman *n*
poor *adj*
popular *adj*
post *v*
post office *n*
postcard *n*
prefer *v*

prepare *v*
prize *n*
problem *n*
programme *n* (US program)
pull *v*
push *v*
pyramid *n*

Q
quarter *n*
queen *n*
quite *adv*

R
race *n* + *v*
railway *n*
ready *adj*
remember *v*
repair *v*
repeat *v*
restaurant *n*
rich *adj*
Richard *n*
right *adj* + *n* (as in direction)
ring *n*
Robert *n*
rocket *n*
rucksack *n* (US backpack)

S
salt *n*
same *adj*
Sarah *n*
save *v*
science *n*
scissors *n*
score *n* + *v*
screen *n*
secret *n*
secretary *n*
sell *v*
send *v*
September *n*
several *adj*
shelf *n*

shorts *n*
should *v*
silver *adj + n*
since *prep*
singer *n*
single *adj*
ski *n + v*
sky *n*
sledge *n + v*
smell *n + v*
snack *n*
snowball *n*
snowboarding *n*
snowman *n*
so *adv + conj*
soap *n*
soft *adj*
somewhere *adv*
soon *adv*
sound *n + v*
south *n*
space *n*
speak *v*
special *adj*
spend *v*
spoon *n*
spot *n*
spotted *adj*
spring *n*
stage *n* (theatre)
stamp *n*
stay *v*
steal *v*
still *adv*
storm *n*
straight on *adv*
strange *adj*
stripe *n*
striped *adj*
student *n*
study *v*
subject *n*
such *det*
suddenly *adv*
sugar *n*
suitcase *n*
summer *n*

sunglasses *n*
sure *adj*
surname *n*
swan *n*
swing *n + v*

T
take *v* (as in time e.g. it takes 20 minutes)
tape recorder *n*
taste *n + v*
taxi *n*
teach *v*
team *n*
telephone *n*
tent *n*
thank *v*
theatre *n*
thousand *n*
through *prep*
tidy *adj + v*
tights *n*
time *n*
timetable *n*
toe *n*
together *adv*
toilet *n*
tomorrow *adv + n*
tonight *adv + n*
torch *n* (US flashlight)
tour *n*
traffic *n*
turn *v*
turn off *v*
turn on *v*
twice *adv*

U
umbrella *n*
unfriendly *adj*
unhappy *adj*
uniform *n*
university *n*
untidy *adj*
until *prep*
unusual *adj*

use *v*
usually *adv*

V
view *n*
violin *n*
visit *v*
volleyball *n*

W
waiter *n*
warm *adj*
way *n*
west *n*
wheel *n*
where *pron*
whisper *v*
whistle *v*
wife *n*
wild *adj*
will *v*
William *n*
win *v*
wing *n*
winner *n*
winter *n*
wish *n + v*
without *prep*
wonderful *adj*
wood *n*
wool *n*
worried *adj*

Y
yet *adv*
you're welcome *excl*
yourself *pron*

Z
zero *n*